Architecture
as Environment

The Grand Tour

Architecture as Environment

Flavio Conti

Translated by Patrick Creagh

HBJ Press
a subsidiary of Harcourt Brace Jovanovich, Inc.
New York

HBJ Press

President, Robert J. George

Publisher, Giles Kemp

Vice President, Richard S. Perkins, Jr.

Managing Director, Valerie S. Hopkins

Executive Editor, Marcia Heath

Series Editor, Carolyn Hall

Staff Editor, Chris Heath

Text Editors: Joelle Delbourgo, Peter Gardner, Amanda Heller, Joyce Milton, Phil Patton

Editorial Production: Karen E. English, Ann McGrath, Eric Brus, Betsie Brownell, Patricia Leal, Pamela George

Project Coordinator, Linda S. Behrens

Business Manager, Edward Koman

Marketing Director, John R. Whitman

Public Relations, Janet Schotta

Business Staff: Pamela Herlich, Joan Kenney

Architectural Consultant, Dennis J. DeWitt

Text Consultants: Janet Adams, Elizabeth R. DeWitt, Perween Hasan

Design Implementation, Designworks

Rizzoli Editore

Authors of the Italian Edition: Dr. Flavio Conti, P. Favole, G. Gattoni, G. M. Tabarelli

Idea and Realization, Harry C. Lindinger

General Supervisor, Luigi U. Re

Graphic Designer, Gerry Valsecchi

Coordinator, Vilma Maggioni

Editorial Supervisor, Gianfranco Malafarina

Research Organizer, Germano Facetti

U.S. Edition Coordinator, Natalie Danesi Murray

Photography Credits:

Carrese: p. 45 bottom, p. 47 bottom left, p. 50 top / *Cauchetier:* p. 82 top left, pp. 73–81, p. 82 bottom, p. 84 / *Gamma-Farza:* pp. 96–98, p. 100 / *Hutchinson:* p. 51 bottom / *Internationales Bildarchiv:* p. 51 top / *Magnum-Bar-AM:* p. 41, p. 45 top right, p. 47 top / *Magnum-Barbey:* pp. 58–61, p. 62 bottom, p. 63, p. 64 top right, p. 64 bottom right, p. 65 top left, p. 65 bottom right, p. 65 bottom middle, p. 65 top right, p. 68 / *Magnum-Berry:* pp. 153–164 / *Magnum-Burri:* p. 52 / *Magnum-Burt Glinn:* p. 57, p. 62 top right, p. 67 / *Magnum-Hopker:* pp. 48–49 / *Magnum-Lessing:* p. 44, p. 50 bottom / *Magnum-Sakura:* pp. 42–43 / *Mangum-Silverstone:* p. 47 bottom right / *M&W Fine Arts:* pp. 121–136, pp. 25–33, p. 34 top, p. 34 bottom left, pp. 35–36 / *Moro:* p. 38, pp. 103–104 / *Rapho-Boireau:* p. 109 bottom / *Rapho-Gerster:* p. 110 top / *Rapho-Koch:* p. 115 top left / *Rapho-Longuepin:* p. 105, p. 109 top / *Rapho-Serraillez:* p. 112, p. 113 top / *Rapho-Silvester:* p. 111 bottom, p. 113 bottom, p. 115 top right, p. 115 bottom / *Rapho-Vuillomenet:* p. 116 / *Rossi:* p. 62 top left, p. 64 top left, p. 64 bottom left, p. 65 bottom left, p. 66, p. 45 top left, p. 46 / *Scala Bencini:* p. 9, p. 15 top / *Scala:* pp. 10–14, p. 15 bottom, pp. 16–20 / *Scarfiotti:* p. 82 middle, p. 82 top right, p. 83 / *Sheridan R.:* p. 34 bottom right / *Sipa-Press:* p. 108 bottom, pp. 89–95, p. 99 / *Stierlin:* pp. 106–107, p. 108 top, p.110 bottom, p. 111 top left, p. 111 top right, p. 114 / *Visalli:* pp. 137–148.

Library of Congress Catalog Card Number: 78-51425
ISBN: 0-15-003728-7

Printed in Italy

Contents

Preface

Architecture as Environment

Architecture is more than the art of constructing individual buildings. It is also the creation of environment. Buildings do not exist in isolation. They not only impose their character on their surroundings but also have an incalculable effect on the lives of the human beings who inhabit them.

A special sense of place and atmosphere distinguishes some cities and places from others and gives them a unique life. Curiously, the city of Machu Picchu, high in the Peruvian Andes, seems far more special to the modern visitor than it was to the Incas who built it. For these Romans of the New World, it was simply one of the defensive outposts of their capital, Cuzco. But the Incan empire vanished under the destructive zeal of the conquistadors, and Machu Picchu alone survived, frozen in time and lost in the green of the sierra. Discovered almost by chance in 1911 by an American named Hiram Bingham, the mountain fortress was recognized as a sort of American Pompeii. This dead city was also a monument, a memorial, in the words of the great Chilean poet Pablo Neruda, to the "dazzling gems and colossal fragments of the lost gods" that sleep under the "imperial ashes" of the New World.

The city of Machu Picchu remains isolated and mysterious in the enchanted green silence of the mountains. Often completely enveloped in clouds, the green-gray stone fortress perches on a damp Andean ridge in the shadow of the granite sugar-loaf peak of Huayna Picchu. In the luminous, mother-of-pearl light, the city seems like the lost world of a dream.

The atmosphere of the city of New Orleans could not be more different. The indolent, refined, and aristocratic Creole city at the mouth of the Mississippi has one of the most inviting of urban landscapes—large, comfortable houses, cool courtyards, and elaborate, wrought-iron balustrades. A melting pot of settlers from France and Spain and slaves from Africa and the Caribbean, New Orleans is one of the most colorful cities in the world, particularly during the festival of Mardi Gras. Honored as the birthplace of jazz and justly famed for its cuisine, it prides itself above all as having successfully transplanted the culture and *savoir vivre* of Old Europe to the soil of the New World.

Back in the Old World stands the ancient city of Salamanca, capital of the old kingdom of León in Spain. With its celebrated university, Roman bridge, Romanesque cathedral, and fine palaces, Salamanca is architecturally enthralling. And above all, there is its Plaza Mayor.

The open-air plaza is the center of life in any Spanish city, reflecting the true face and personality of its people. It is the place to meet and gossip and pass the time of day; to conduct business; and, in times past, to hold bullfights and *autos-da-fé*, the pyres that burned the victims of the Inquisition. The architect Alberto de Churriguera, one of the famous family of artists, built at Salamanca one of the most beautiful plazas in all of Spain. The vast square, with its deep arcades and delicate balconies, is at once peaceful and dramatic—a place for quiet reflection as well as festivity and celebration.

The center of Dubrovnik, which also basks in the hot Mediterranean sun, is perhaps less imposing than that of Salamanca. Known as the Stradun, it is a sunny, broad corridor that crosses the town from east to west. The town itself is one of the most captivating in the Adriatic. Its mighty defensive walls and towers still dominate the blue sea from which for centuries it drew its life, wealth, and glory.

The proud city that for a thousand years had the freedom of the seas and dealt on equal terms with the greatest powers of Europe is today a thriving tourist resort. But its nobility lives on, not only in the fine palaces and magnificent churches but also in the atmosphere of the town—a sea-beaten rock transformed into a picturesque pocket of civilization.

With its harsh climate and gray buildings, Dublin has a distinctly un-Mediterranean character. James Joyce, more than any other writer, is the bard of Dublin; and readers the world over now see the city through his eyes, recognizing the squalor that exists alongside its romantic aspect. Joyce's name for it—"dear dirty Dublin"—expresses his ambivalence toward his home city. His writing exposes the problems of urbanization and nationalism and the effects of the industrial revolution on a backward agricultural country. But above all, he shows us the soul, the hopes, the myths, and the nightmares of the Irish people. It is worth the trouble of seeking out Joyce's Dublin, for it ranks among the most fascinating and elusive of landscapes.

The unprepossessing appearance of the Wailing Wall—those few, fire-damaged, time-eroded stones—belies the full weight of its historic and religious dimension. Yet, it is all that remains of the Second Temple of Jerusalem. A thousand years before the words of the Prophet resounded at Mecca, it stood at the center of a small but tenacious nation. Its founding fathers had paid in blood and tears for that land and were determined to bind their destiny to it forever. They built a temple to their god, which stood as the symbol of their traditions and their unity as a people. Centuries later the Jewish people are still committed to the few rows of stones that carry the memory of Solomon's nation into the twentieth century.

The value of the Kaaba at Mecca is perhaps best expressed by the endless lines of white-robed pilgrims visiting the sanctuary. They arrive there by all available means and at whatever cost, from all corners of the Islamic world. What they come to see is physically unremarkable: a cube of stones and an arcaded courtyard. For countless centuries, the Kaaba—a

meeting place for the people of Arabia—had been sacred long before the coming of the Prophet, linking the pilgrim with his heritage as well as with his god.

The special atmosphere of Marrakesh, however, belongs very definitely to the present, not the past. Certainly the city has a splendid history, to which its mosques and palaces and gates are an eloquent memorial. But today, its squares and markets, mosques, and gardens are crowded with people from all over the world. Marrakesh is like an endlessly exuberant meeting place—"Capital of the South," folk festival center of North Africa, hippie mecca. But notwithstanding the influx of tourists, the people of Marrakesh still retain many of their ancient traditions. Their heritage, like the architecture of the city, lives on—and in the theater of Marrakesh, the play is perhaps even more immediately fascinating than the scenery.

At first sight, the busy crowds which bargain and quarrel in the narrow streets of the Old City of Damascus seem very similar to those of Marrakesh. And yet the mood of the city stems from a different past. If the Moroccan city is the Capital of the South, Damascus is the gateway to Mecca and to the Mediterranean. The religions and the empires that have passed through this land—Egyptian, Assyrian, Persian, Macedonian, Roman, Byzantine, Arab, Crusader, Turkish, Jewish—have all left their traces. On the road to Damascus, Saint Paul was converted. The great Sala-

din established religious colleges in the city and finally retired there in 1192. History and politics, cultures and religions are interwoven in its cosmopolitan atmosphere. Once proud of its opulent beauty, which earned it the name of al-Fayha (the Fragrant One), the city is still justly proud of its ancient crafts, such as the damask cloth and the damascened blades that are still found in the *souks* (markets) today.

When the Moors gained control of the city of Cordova in the eighth century A.D., they planned to build the most impressive mosque in the world; and the Great Mosque, with its infinite series of columns and splendidly worked arches, became one of the glories of Islamic architecture. When the Christians took the city, the mosque—now put to use as a cathedral—was at first scrupulously preserved. After three centuries, however, a large Romanesque church was inserted into the center of the vast Moslem structure. But the addition enhances the interest of the monument as a whole. The contradictions inherent in the structure of the building demonstrate both the dissimilarities and the likenesses between its Moorish and Christian builders.

Such architectural adaptations bring buildings to life, expressing the emotions—the faiths and hopes, the joys and sorrows—of humanity. For not even the most brilliant architects can infuse their creations with life: It requires the mediating forces of cultures and time to do that.

Dubrovnik

Yugoslavia

Preceding page, the major harbor of Old Ragusa, seen from the southeast. The triple arches of the port mark the site of the channel which originally divided the Latin island republic of Ragusa from the Slavic settlement—Dubrovnik—on the mainland.

Facing page, a western view of the Lovrijenac Fort (Fort of St. Lawrence) from the city walls. The walls reach a thickness of 18 feet and a maximum height of 72 feet, with 17 towers, 5 bastions, and a major fortress. No traffic is permitted within the city walls.

Above, the massive walls which enclose the oldest part of the town.

Above right, the fourteenth-century Pile Gate, the western gate of the city. Above the portal is a statue of Saint Blaise, the patron saint of the city, holding a model of Ragusa in his left hand.

Right, the Dominican monastery overlooking the old harbor, which is now used only for fishing boats and pleasure craft. The breakwater was built in the fifteenth century by Paskoje Miličević.

Ragusa was originally a rugged, hilly island, and Old Ragusa is built atop its steep elevations, with its various levels connected with flights of stairs (left).

Right, the round Minčeta tower with the Jesuit convent and the Collegium Ragusinum in the background. The tower was once square, but its shape was altered in the fifteenth century to strengthen it against the new threat presented by firearms. It was redesigned by the architects Michelozzo and Juraj Dalmatinac.

Below right, a view of Dubrovnik from the northern walls. The fifteenth-century stone houses have three or four one-room floors. They were originally roofed with thatch and straw, but in the thirteenth century, the government insisted that all roofs be made of tile as a protection against fire. Beyond the city lies the Adriatic and the island of Lokrum, where Richard the Lion-Hearted was shipwrecked on his return from Palestine in 1192. Richard vowed to build a church to Saint Mary on the spot, but he was persuaded by the Ragusans to erect it instead in their city. The church was destroyed by the earthquake of 1667.

Above left, a view of the Stradun, the old city's main street. Originally the canal separating the island of Ragusa from the mainland, it was filled in during the thirteenth century as the city of Ragusa expanded.

Above, a view looking eastward from the Stradun. The monument to the left is Roland's column, which was placed there in 1418. It was used by the town crier when he announced senate decisions, and it also flew the flag of the republic.

Left, the façade of the Rector's Palace, which is located on the north side of the Stradun. One of the town's largest buildings, it was first built in the twelfth century. Severely damaged by earthquakes, the palace was rebuilt in the fifteenth century, and the style is a mixture of late Romanesque (the ground floor arcade) and late Gothic (the top floor windows).

Right, the Church of St. Blaise, at the eastern end of the Stradun. The original church burned down in 1706 and was rebuilt in the Baroque style. Directly in front of the church is Roland's column.

Below, the Dominican monastery and church, dating from the fourteenth and fifteenth centuries. Originally outside the walls, it was enclosed within the new fortifications of the mid-fifteenth century.

Below right, a fifteenth-century fountain by Onofrio de la Cava, an Italian architect who helped build the city walls. He also completed an aqueduct in 1438, which supplied the city with greatly needed fresh water and still feeds the fountain today. In the background is the Sponza Palace, built in the 1520s in a mixture of Gothic and Renaissance styles.

Above left, the interior courtyard of the Rector's Palace. The Renaissance arcade shows the influence of the Italian architect Michelozzo. The bust at the foot of the stairs is of Miho Pracat, a rich merchant who left his wealth to the state.

Above, two of the columns supporting the façade of the Rector's Palace, and a detail of a third (near right). Though its shaft is simple, the capital depicts—in exquisite detail—some peasants bringing gifts to the god Aesculapius.

Left, another view of Onofrio de la Cava's fountain at the eastern end of the plaza.

Facing page, above right, a pietà over the south door of the Franciscan church with Saint Jerome on the left and Saint John the Baptist on the right. Far right, coupled columns in the oldest cloister of the Franciscan monastery. They are the work of Miho from Bar in Montenegro. The slippage of masonry in the left capital was presumably caused by an earthquake.

Following page, Dubrovnik, "the pearl of the Adriatic." One of the most beautiful places on the Dalmatian coast, it is known as "the Slav Athens."

Dubrovnik Yugoslavia

The picturesque city of Dubrovnik, on the southern Adriatic coast of Yugoslavia, is primarily a port and tourist center. Jutting out into the sea under the bare limestone mass of Mount Srdj, the city retains the flavor of its past, with its fortifications and medieval architecture and its houses of perfectly fitted square stones. It is a city of palaces and gardens, paved narrow alleys opening out into luminous squares, and cool, shadowy churches ornamented with paintings by Titian and Pordenone.

All bear witness to a time when Dubrovnik was a powerful merchant republic and center of Serbo-Croatian culture. Trade brought commercial prosperity as well as cultural contributions from the greatest masters. Merchants came from every part of Europe and the Mediterranean to buy or sell, to make a bargain or sign a contract. Today, the cosmopolitan spirit of the past lives on in the form of tourists, with their different styles of dress and their different languages. Owing to the stream of travelers who explore the city each year, modern Dubrovnik is as lively, if not as prosperous, as it was at the height of its power.

Seen from the air, the Dalmatian coast appears as a lace work of islands, peninsulas, and sheltered bays, fringing the blue-green Adriatic Sea. But in reality, there is nothing delicate about this coast-line, which is composed of rugged mountains, rocky promontories, and dry, infertile land. It is habitable only by a sturdy people.

Such were the original inhabitants who came, around A.D. 615, from Epidaurus some fifteen miles to the south. Epidaurus, the site of modern Cavtat, had originally been a Greek colony, which later became Roman. When it was destroyed by the Slavs and Avars, the survivors fled north to settle on the small rocky island called Ragusa. They continued, however, to regard themselves as part of the Byzantine Empire.

The island of Ragusa was then separated from the mainland by a channel of water at its north end. On the fringes of the oak forests on the mainland opposite the island, there grew up a Slavic settlement called Dubrovnik *(dubrava* in Serbo-Croatian means "wood"). The Ragusans built their earliest defensive walls facing the mainland, though nothing remains of the original stacked stone and wood they used. Fortified repeatedly as the city grew, Ragusa was always best protected on its north side.

Though the Ragusans took care to protect themselves from their Slavic neigh-

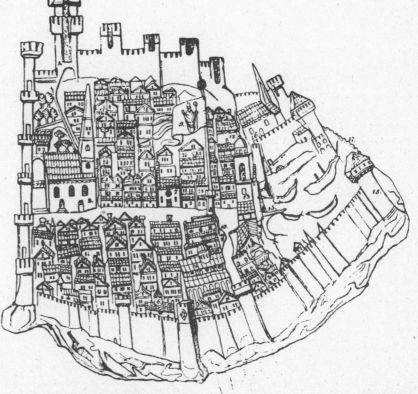

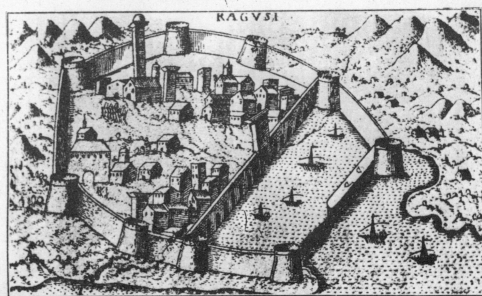

Above right, Ragusa in about 1485, showing the Minčeta Tower and the Stradun. A plate from 1580 (right) shows the harbor fortifications of the early fourteenth century.

Above, the arms of the Republic of Ragusa.

Below, a seventeenth-century print showing Ragusa from the west.

Above, a painting of the city made shortly before the earthquake of April 6, 1667.

bors, they also recognized the value of diplomacy. Having no cultivable land on their rocky island, they offered payment to the Slavs in return for the use of crop land. In deference to the authority of Byzantium, they secured permission for this arrangement from Emperor Basil I in the second half of the ninth century. They continued to pay this tribute of thirty-six golden nomismata a year, until the arrival of the Ottoman Turks several centuries later.

From the start, the Ragusans turned to the sea for their livelihood. Good seamen and even better merchants, they made their presence felt in every port in the Mediterranean. The sea, however, was not without its dangers. During the ninth century, the maritime freedom of the Ragusans was threatened by Arabs from southern Italy. From their base at Bari, the Arabs controlled the Strait of Otranto, the channel linking the Ionian and Adriatic seas, and on one occasion they blockaded the Ragusans for fifteen months. Afterward, the Ragusans joined forces with the Frankish army in a campaign which even-

tually broke the Arab's control of Mediterranean commerce.

The Ragusans, however, were a peace-loving people, preferring to seek independence through wealth rather than war. When Venice attacked Croatia in 1000, the Ragusans decided to accept Venetian jurisdiction while still recognizing Byzantine sovereignty. Four centuries later, the Ragusan skill at negotiation had become legend. In the words of Filippe de Diversis, rector of the local school: "We make every effort to be at peace with everyone and, as far as possible, to avoid conflicts and wars, by using great patience and above all a great deal of money."

Ragusa's size, wealth, and power grew steadily. During the eleventh century, the

town greatly expanded, and for the first time, its inhabitants moved out of their bastioned city on the rock to establish new walls on a steep, high rock west of the city itself. By the twelfth century, the narrow channel separating Ragusa and Dubrovnik was filled in, and the defensive walls were again extended and enlarged.

The growing merchant city-state of Ragusa-Dubrovnik recognized Venetian suzerainty in 1205. They were to continue to accept Venetian rule until 1358, even though Ragusa achieved a prosperity and independence which at times exerted a commercial and diplomatic influence rivaling that of its suzerain. Rather than regarding Ragusa as a rival, the Venetians recognized its importance as a valuable trading base with the Balkan hinterland.

Right, the Stradun, the main street of Ragusa, in the nineteenth century. Behind the Rector's Palace, at the right, is the Sponza Palace. The many levels of Dubrovnik are connected by flights of winding stairs (below, far right). Below right, a characteristic view of the old city.

Goods prized throughout Europe passed through the Ragusan port: honey, wax, wood, leather, silver, copper, minerals, iron, lead, cattle, and—not the least profitable—slaves from Bosnia and Herzegovina, brought to market by their own princes greedy for the fine craftsmanship of European goods.

Ragusa's wealth found a natural outlet in building projects. Besides renewing and reinforcing the ramparts, the town leaders commissioned magnificent public buildings. Indeed, the Rector's Palace, begun in the twelfth century and rebuilt in the fifteenth, is considered one of the masterpieces of Dalmatian architecture.

Two monasteries, one Franciscan and the other Dominican, were built in the fourteenth century. The lower cloister of the former, a late Romanesque work, was sculpted by Miho Brajkav. A pharmacy, the oldest in Europe, opened in this cloister in 1317 and is still in operation. The upper cloister of the monastery is an elegant Gothic structure.

During the thirteenth century, the new part of the city took on its distinctive form. In contrast to the older parts of the city, where dwellings were crowded together and deprived of light and air, its network of narrow streets was flooded with light reflected from the rows of white limestone façades.

Of all the structures in Dubrovnik, the most dramatic—and most characteristic—are the city walls. These massive fortifications not only reflect the prudent Ragusan temperament but also set the architectural tone of the city, preserving its quaint unity and compactness.

By the mid-fourteenth century, the entire city was surrounded by a wall averaging five feet thick, with thirteen tall, square towers. By the mid-fifteenth century, the walls reached their greatest size. A section

approximately one mile in length is preserved today.

The town and its ramparts are indivisible. Most immediately striking, whether approaching the city by sea or by land, is the geometric rhythm of the city walls, with their square towers. The mightiest of all is the massive cylinder on the northwest corner of the walls known as the Minčeta Tower. Begun in 1319, it is the linchpin of the defensive system. Another support is provided by the Lovrijenac Fort (Fort of St. Lawrence) which stands outside the wall on the rock west of the city as well as the narrow monolithic fortress tower called the Revelin, at the northeast corner of the city. For all their appreciation of money, the Ragusans also valued their independence, as exhibited by their selec-

tion for the inscription over the entrance to the Lovrijenac Fort: "Freedom is not sold for all the gold in the world."

In February 1358, Venice signed the Zadar Peace Treaty relinquishing control of Dalmatia to Hungary. A few months later, however, the Ragusans, with exemplary diplomatic wisdom, negotiated the Treaty of Visegrad, which allowed them complete independence from Hungary. Recognizing the growing power of the Ottoman Empire, the Ragusans signed a trade agreement with the Turks as early as 1396. In this way, they insured for themselves the prosperous role of middlemen between the Balkans and Europe, despite the fact that they were under Turkish domination.

The fifteenth and sixteenth centuries constituted a golden age for Ragusa. The number of ships in the Ragusan fleet rose to 180. Trading vessels came from Dalmatia, Italy, Greece, Sicily, and even France and Spain—so many that they were often forced to wait in a bay of the small nearby island of Lokrum before being allowed to enter the harbor.

Meanwhile, the Ragusans were constantly searching for ways to improve and embellish their city and its environment. During the fourteenth century, for example, they had established building standards which decreed that fire-prone wooden houses should be replaced by stone ones. They welcomed foreign artists who added a Renaissance sensibility—which had been maturing on the opposite shore of the Adriatic—to the typically Venetian Gothic buildings.

Gold and jewelry were an important part of Ragusan dress, and wealthy connoisseurs supported the local goldsmiths and craftsmen who created objects of rare beauty. Chalices, cups, ciboria, enameled reliquaries, bowls, crosses, weapons, medallions, and statues of saints—such local works were given as tribute by the city to the potentates of Europe. Religious articles were especially popular because Ragusa was an important point on the route of pilgrims journeying to Palestine.

The arrival of big European fleets in the Mediterranean created competition for Dubrovnik, and the discovery of America slowly began to shift the whole axis of European trade. Most important, the internal decay of the Ottoman Empire led to corruption, insecurity, and economic decline in the Balkan markets. A slow decline was destined for Ragusa.

Moreover, the city suffered a natural disaster. On April 6, 1667, an earthquake destroyed much of the lower part of Ragusa. The material damage, however, was fairly easily repaired. The old layout of the town was respected, and the only changes consisted of some Baroque additions.

The loss of human life was far more serious. About four thousand people perished, including large numbers of the old Latin patrician families. As a result, the governing board of the city was greatly weakened.

The earthquake meant the end of Ragusa's former Latin culture. People of Slavic origin came from the surrounding country, and a new local culture gradually developed, in which the Slavic elements eventually predominated. Some 150 years later, the pacific citizens of Ragusa were quietly deprived of their independence. In May 1806, the government of Ragusa allowed Napoleon's troops free passage through their city—the first foreign army to enter Ragusa. But the army stayed. Two years later, the French Marshal Marmont officially informed the Ragusan government that their state had ceased to exist.

The old republican liberties were never regained. On Napoleon's fall, the Congress of Vienna (1815) assigned the city to Austria. Then, in 1918, Dubrovnik became a part of the newly created state of Yugoslavia.

Above right, women in traditional, long white chemise-frocks, which are often paired with brightly colored, embroidered waistcoats called jeleks.

Above far right, a religious procession in Dubrovnik. For festivals, the men wear baggy blue trousers, white shirts, and decorative jeleci *(vests).*

Right, an old view of the main square.

The Great Mosque at Cordova

Spain

Preceding page, the Great Mosque of Cordova, La Mezquita, seen from near the Calahorra Tower. Facing page, the Gate of the Palms, main entrance to the prayer hall. The decoration over the arch is Christian. Above, a corner of the Patio de los Naranjos (Court of the Oranges). Right, the Gate of the Pardon, main entrance to the mosque, built in Moorish style in 1377. Below, the Christian tower over the Gate of the Pardon which replaced the original minaret.

Above right, the sixteenth-century Gothic cathedral rising incongruously from the midst of the Moslem prayer hall. The mosque was enlarged three times to accommodate worshipers. In the foreground is the Gate of the Palms and the north side of the hall. In the middle of the tenth century, this hall was strengthened with pillars and horseshoe arches to support the aisles, which had become dangerously extended.

Above left, buttresses of the cathedral. Left, clerestory windows that were added around the cathedral.

Right and far right, views of the arcade that surrounds the courtyard.

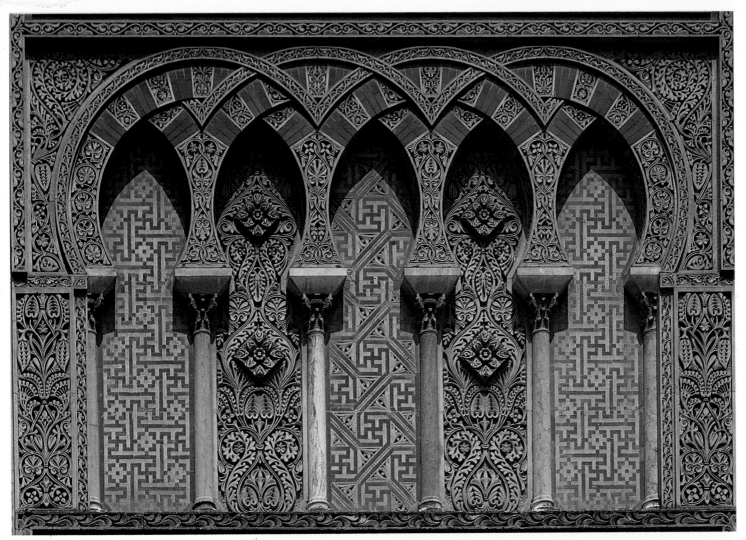

Facing page, an elaborate portal of the eastern façade. It was constructed between 987 and 988 by al-Mansur, who was responsible for the last and most extensive enlargement of the mosque. Flanking the portal are fine examples of scalloped arches, stone lattices, and double-arched niches. Fretted (or stepped) crenelations surmount the façade.

Above, blind arches over one of the entrances in the mosque's western façade, dating from the time of al-Hakam II (961–976). The patterned tilework and floral bas-reliefs, in which simple motifs are elaborated and repeated, are characteristic of the art of the caliphate. Islamic theology condemned realistic representations of nature. Right, Gothic ornamentation of the late fifteenth century added to an existing doorway. This is the Postigo de Palacio (Palace Gate), near the southwest corner of the mosque.

Above left, slender columns supporting heavy piers, which are joined by two tiers of banded arches. These arches lend unity to the often dissimilar columns and capitals. The aisles appear austere in comparison to the dome of al-Hakam's maqsura (far left) with its elegant ribs and delicate mosaics. To help support the weight of the dome, cross-bracing arches (left) were inserted into the arches beneath it. These are both decorative and functional.

Above right, foiled arches of the Chapel of Villaviciosa, the second mihrab to be built. Right, decoration above one of the doors leading to al-Hakam's mihrab. The mosaics here, as on the dome to the left, are said to have been the work of Byzantine craftsmen.

Following page, a view from the tower of the eastern half of the mosque and the cathedral.

The Great Mosque At Cordova Spain

It's hard to imagine that the quiet provincial town of Cordova in southern Spain was once the largest city in Europe, after Constantinople, and the intellectual and cultural center of the West. During the years of Moslem dominion in Spain, which extended from the middle of the eighth century to the early eleventh, Cordova was famed for its scholars, physicians, and poets, its silks and leatherwork, and its magnificent buildings. Arab historians claim that at the height of its power the city was twenty-four miles long by six miles wide and had over 250,000 buildings, including 3,000 mosques, palaces, and baths.

The flavor of Moslem Cordova lingers on in the low, whitewashed houses, tiny squares, narrow streets, and flower-filled windowsills of today's town. But its architectural monuments have all been reduced to ruins—with one exception. The Great Mosque, known locally as La Mezquita, was once the largest mosque in existence. Today, it is the third largest and is still—despite some regrettable Christian alterations made in the sixteenth century—one of the glories of Islamic architecture.

The mosque was begun in A.D. 785 by the Emir Abd al-Rahman I and was frequently enlarged and embellished over the following two hundred years by his successors. To accommodate the growing population of Cordova, the mosque was enlarged four times, although always in conformity with the original conception. The final structure represents a triumph of unity and a signal proof of the Moslem flair for creative adaptation. Because the earliest parts of the mosque predate the development of various schools of Islamic architecture, they also embody some characteristics of the monuments of the Classical Western world.

Abd al-Rahman was a member of the Umayyad dynasty, which ruled the Moslem empire from soon after the death of Mohammed in 632 until 750. At that time, the Umayyads were bloodily overthrown by their rivals, the Abbasids, who moved the capital from Damascus to Baghdad. The fugitive Abd al-Rahman settled in Cordova in 756, established his leadership over Spain's Arab aristocracy, and made Cordova the capital of an independent emirate that acknowledged the supremacy of Baghdad only in matters of religion.

The site Abd al-Rahman chose for his mosque—in the center of the city on the right bank of the Guadalquivir River—was already occupied by a Visigothic church. Moslems and Christians had, in fact, prayed side by side in adjoining halves of the church since 748. In 785, Abd al-Rahman purchased the Christian half of the church and tore down much of the build-

Cordova was a lively cultural center in Europe during the early Middle Ages. The thirteenth-century miniature (above right), which is probably Syrian, depicts a distinctly Western scene: the Athenian lawgiver Solon with three disciples. Right, a nineteenth-century engraving of the maqsura, *showing the* mihrab *in the center of the wall.*

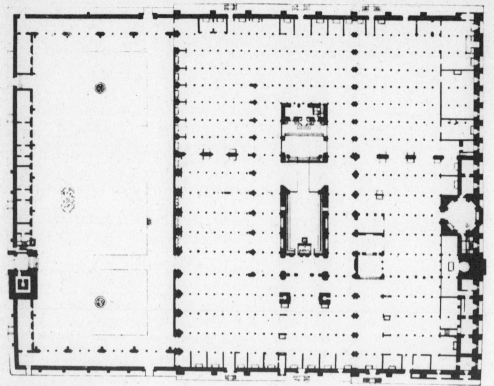

Above, a ground plan of the mosque as it stands today. The sixteenth-century cathedral rises out of the center of the prayer hall, surrounded by some eight hundred pillars.

Right, one of the arches separating the courtyard from the prayer hall.

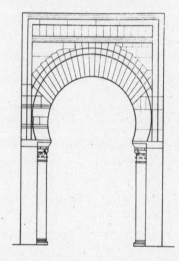

Intersecting arches like those used for al-Hakam's maqsura *(above right) are Eastern in origin.*

Right, a miniature showing a building in Moslem Cordova covered with multicolored tiles. The decoration is common in Islamic architecture, especially in Eastern countries such as Syria and Persia.

ing. Because he encouraged the construction to be completed in only twelve months, it was necessary to assimilate the orientation of the structure of the original Visigothic church in the new mosque.

The mosque's basic plan was simple. It consisted of a large rectangular enclosure divided into an open courtyard and a slightly larger prayer hall on the south side. The hall had eleven parallel aisles ending in a south wall, or *qibla.* Moslem tradition dictates that *qibla* walls face Mecca (in this case, east-southeast), but as the foundation of the original church was used for the mosque, the *qibla* here faces south. The central aisle, wider than the rest, terminated in a *mihrab,* a concave niche cut into the *qibla.* The *mihrab,* found

in all mosques, directs the eyes and thoughts of the worshipers toward Mecca.

The columns used in the mosque were made of jasper, marble, and other fine stone. Most had been pillaged from Roman and Visigothic monuments as far away as North Africa and the town of Narbonne in France. Others came from the original church itself. The area of the roof was so extensive that the mosque would have seemed oppressively low had the pillars been used just as they were. Abd al-Rahman's architect solved the problem by placing massive rectangular pillars atop the capitals of the columns. These upper pillars were joined at the top, beneath the flat-beamed roof, by rounded arches composed of alternating bands of

white stone and red brick. As reinforcement, the architect added a subsidiary series of similarly banded arches just above the abacuses (the slabs on top of the capitals). These two-tiered arches, possibly inspired by Roman aqueducts (such as the one at Merida), produce a stunning aesthetic effect.

The next emir, Abd al-Rahman II (822–852), enlarged the mosque. Though he spent much of his reign fighting Christians from the northern provinces of the peninsula and suppressing rebellious Arab chieftains nearer home, he was of a more pacific nature than some of his predecessors. He also had a taste for magnificence that prompted him not simply to rival but to outdo the court at Baghdad. He included scholars, poets, and dancing girls in his entourage and used his fabulous wealth to promote commerce and patronize the arts.

Abd al-Rahman II pulled down the mosque's *qibla* wall, added eight bays to the existing aisles, and transferred the original *mihrab*, somewhat enlarged, to a new *qibla*. His successor, Abu Abdallah Mohammed I (852–856), is credited with constructing the mosque's *maqsura*, which literally means "closed-off space." This prayer enclosure, reserved exclusively for Moslem rulers, is surrounded by windowed walls for security from assassins.

Abd al-Rahman III, the caliph of Moslem Spain from 912 to 961, also left his mark on the mosque. In many respects comparable to Louis XIV, he ruled Islamic Spain in the extravagant manner of a grand monarch, although he was not always entirely successful in subduing the country's dissident elements. He was responsible for erecting a minaret over the Great Mosque's main entrance, the Gate of the Pardon. He also strengthened the north side of the prayer hall and surrounded the courtyard with arcades.

The most beautiful additions to the mosque were undertaken by al-Hakam II, who was caliph from 961 to 976. Known as the "Scholar King," the caliph demonstrated a greater interest in the arts and sciences than any of his predecessors. He pierced Abd al-Rahman's *qibla* with lofty horseshoe and multifoil arches—the first to have real constructional value in Islamic architecture. He then lengthened the aisles by adding another twelve bays to the previous twenty. In his new *qibla*, he constructed a third *mihrab*, larger and far more ornate than the previous two, and in front of it built another *maqsura* which consisted of three domed bays. He also added a dome to what was probably Abd al-Rahman's *mihrab* and is now known as

Throughout the early Middle Ages—the Dark Ages of European history—Arab scientists were outstanding in many fields, including medicine. Above right, a surgeon replacing a dislocated shoulder. Right, an astronomer using a sextant to observe the course of a comet.

the Chapel of Villaviciosa.

Al-Hakam's *mihrab* and *maqsura* are the crowning glory of the mosque. Until the construction of the Alhambra in Granada three hundred years later, no surviving examples of Western Islamic architecture could compare with their refined elegance. The outer face of the *mihrab*, like the central dome of the *maqsura*, is covered with splendid mosaics, the work of Byzantine craftsmen. The *mihrab* itself is a heptagonal chamber, with a fluted dome molded into the shape of a shell and marble-lined walls richly sculpted with plant motifs.

The four large domes are masterpieces, each one supported by paired ribs laid in crisscross fashion to form an octagonal star pattern. To further secure these heavy vaults, al-Hakam's architect strengthened the two-tiered arches beneath them by adding interlocking arches with decorative, scalloped profiles. The elaborate, interwoven ribs of the vaults themselves so took the fancy of later European architects that they served as the inspiration for many similar Baroque constructions.

The last Moslem to enlarge the mosque was al-Mansur, an ambitious minister who usurped power soon after the death of al-

At the time the mosque was built, Cordova was the most important center of medical, historical, and astronomical studies in Western Europe. This page, illustrations from early manuscripts. Above, The Pharmacy *(1224); left,* The Physician Andromakhos Watches Agricultural Activities *(1119); right,* Dioscorides and Student *(1200). Here, the Greek physician Dioscorides shows a mandrake to one of his disciples.*

cathedral's chapter to tear down part of the mosque to erect a new cathedral within. When he saw the outcome of his unfortunate decision, Charles expressed regret for it in words that history can only endorse: "You have built what you and others might have built anywhere, but you have destroyed something that is unique in the world."

Yet the cathedral, which extends across eight of the nineteen aisles in the prayer hall, has impaired—but not destroyed—the mosque's subtle harmony. Today, it is common to enter by the elaborately decorated Gate of the Pardon and cross the sunny Patio de los Naranjos (Court of the Oranges), with its tall palms, fountains, and the orange trees that give it its name. You then enter a somber forest of many-hued columns which, with their seemingly

Hakam and made an unsuccessful attempt to found his own dynasty. Because the population of Cordova had expanded considerably by this time, the mosque could no longer hold the crowds of worshipers who came for Friday prayers. Unable to extend the prayer hall to the south because of the proximity of the river, al-Mansur added eight aisles to the east and, at the same time, enlarged the courtyard so that the entire structure retained its rectangular shape.

Al-Mansur was a man of many faces—extremely devout, a mystic, a masterly general, and a powerful ruler. But his

devastating raids across the northern Christian provinces and his violent suppression of factious Arab chiefs presaged the end of the caliphate. In 1032, thirty years after his death, al-Mansur's empire disintegrated into a federation of petty states.

Moslem power steadily waned during the next two centuries, and in 1236, Cordova fell into Christian hands. The Great Mosque was immediately adopted as a cathedral. However, apart from the addition of a Gothic choir in about 1260, it remained intact until 1533, when the Holy Roman Emperor Charles V permitted the

infinite interplay of banded arches, suggest the palms of a desert oasis. You can admire the *maqsura* and the stuccoed dome of the *mihrab*. Then suddenly, you come upon the cathedral, full of light and heavy with incense.

The cathedral can be seen as a disfigurement, an intrusion upon the architectural unity of the mosque. In a philosophical sense, the transformation of the Great Mosque represents the clash of two diverse cultures and religions—of West and East. Given the history of post-Reconquest Spain, we are perhaps fortunate to have been left with so much.

The Wailing Wall

Jerusalem

As they have for centuries, Jews still gather at the Wailing Wall to pray. The Holy Square (preceding page) is a recent addition to the site, replacing the narrow alley that used to run along the wall. It functions as a sort of outdoor synagogue. Huge blocks of Herodian masonry (facing page) stand in mute testimony to ancient engineering. No mortar joins the massive stones, which measure up to ten feet in length. Above, an old man wearing the traditional yarmulke, or skull cap. Jewish custom requires men to cover their heads at the wall as a sign of respect. Right, Jews wearing the tallith, or prayer shawl, and carrying branches in celebration of Sukkoth, the harvest festival. Below, Jews in Chassidic dress, which is derived from costumes of eighteenth-century Poland, where this ultraorthodox sect originated.

The Wailing Wall is a great tourist attraction (far left and below left) for Jews of all nations. In deference to religious law, taking photographs is barred on the Sabbath. Oblivious to tourists, a single Chassid (left) stands absorbed in prayer.

Right, a Yemeni Jew, performing a ritual dance of celebration before the Wailing Wall. His colorful dress symbolizes Joseph's "coat of many colors." Below, men reading prayer books before a canopy veiling the Torah, the holy scrolls on which the first five books of the Old Testament are handwritten. As in Orthodox synagogues, women pray separately (below right). Strict Orthodox Jewish women shave their heads at marriage and, thereafter, reveal their heads only to their husbands.

The Wailing Wall, as it is known in English, was named after the laments uttered there for the destruction of the Second Temple of Jerusalem. Its Hebrew name, however, is Kotel Maaravi (Western Wall). This recalls its original function as part of the retaining wall surrounding the Second Temple, built in the sixth century B.C. Preceding page, worshipers standing in the shadow of a Menorah, the traditional branched candlestick.

Above left, Chassidim at prayer. Left, the excavations of "Robinson's arch," discovered by Dr. Edward Robinson in 1968. The row of stones protruding from the wall is thought to have supported the springing of an arch, which spanned a paved street. The arch was part of a bridge which connected the temple with the Upper City.

Above, the Triple Gate, built by Herod, which stood over one of the portals leading into the temple enclosure. It was blocked by the Crusaders. Right, a wooden fence dividing male and female worshipers.

Following page, visitors and pilgrims converge at the Wailing Wall.

The Wailing Wall Jerusalem

Among the hundreds of religious monuments in Jerusalem, the Wailing Wall stands out, stark and unadorned. These ancient, weathered stones mark the holiest site on earth for Jews throughout the world, for they are all that remain of the Second Temple of Jerusalem, which was destroyed in A.D. 70. Known to the ancient Jews as the Western Wall, it was dubbed the Wailing Wall by European travelers who witnessed the mournful vigils of the pious before its stones. Throughout almost two thousand years of oppression and exile, Jewish pilgrims have sought out the Wailing Wall, to mourn the loss of their beloved homeland. Their pilgrimages reaffirm the traditional belief that "the Divine Presence never departs from the Western Wall."

The Second Temple stood at the heart of the religious life of the ancient Jews. Here, where only the ritually pure could enter, sacrifices were offered to their god Yahweh by the hereditary priests; here, the Great Sanhedrin, the supreme council of religious lawmakers, had its seat; and here, Jews from all over Israel gathered to celebrate the three great festivals of the year.

About 1300 B.C., Moses led the Hebrews out of Egypt and slavery in search of the Promised Land. They returned to their ancestral homeland of Canaan, now Israel, where centuries before they had lived as seminomads along with many other Semitic tribes. The reconquest of Canaan took centuries, and decisive victory came only under King David at the start of the first millenium B.C. David's triumph over the Philistines, who dominated the coast, is immortalized in the story of David and Goliath, while his defeat of the Jebusites, who controlled the interior, gave the Jews a new capital city—the Jebusite fortress of Jerusalem.

When David captured Jerusalem, the Jews had no religious buildings. Although his people now lived in houses, Yahweh himself still led a nomadic existence. His symbolic home was a tent, the Tabernacle, in which was kept the Ark of the Covenant, a small box thought to contain the

Above left, a nineteenth-century map of Jerusalem showing what is now known as the Old City. The Wailing Wall lies along the western side of the Haram esh Sharif, a sacred complex of mosques. Above, Jerusalem, shown in an illuminated manuscript of the fifteenth century. Left, Jerusalem seen from the Garden of Gethsemane, at the foot of the Mount of Olives. In the center is one of the city's oldest Moslem buildings, the Dome of the Rock.

ing to First Chronicles, this was because David's warring had "shed much blood upon the earth," making him unfit to be the builder of the house of God.

This honor went instead to David's son, Solomon. While David was a warrior,

The temple took seven years to build and was finally completed around 960 B.C. In solemn procession the people conducted the ark to its new home, where a white-robed choir and an orchestra of harps, cymbals, and trumpets made holy music, and prodigious numbers of sheep and oxen were sacrificed as peace offerings. When the Ark of the Covenant had been placed in the innermost shrine, "The house of the Lord was filled with a cloud, so that the priests could not stand to minister . . . for the glory of the Lord had filled the house of God" (2 Chron. 5:13–14).

Biblical descriptions give a general idea of what the temple must have looked like. Situated on Mount Moriah (where its proximity to Solomon's palace has prompted some scholars to see it as a kind of royal chapel), it faced east, toward the rising sun. Designed in the Phoenician manner, which may be seen as a provincial version of the Egyptian style, the temple was constructed on ascending levels and was thus also reminiscent of the ziggurats (terraced temples) of Mesopotamia. Its three rooms, arranged in a long rectangle facing a courtyard, suggested the ordinary Semitic house—a reminder, perhaps, that the temple was, after all, the house of God. In the courtyard stood the altar for animal sacrifice and a huge bowl, more than sixteen feet across, called the Brazen Sea, which the priests used for purification rites.

Above, an archway spanning the Via Dolorosa, or Way of the Cross, along which Jesus is believed to have passed on his way to Golgotha and his crucifixion.

Right, a characteristically tortuous Old City street, overhung with picturesque balconies.

tablets on which Moses had written the Ten Commandments. With great pomp and ceremony, David conveyed the Ark of the Covenant to Jerusalem, where a splendid new Tabernacle had been prepared for it.

But the way of life symbolized by the portable ark was passing. The Jews were no longer a loose confederation of tribes but a united kingdom. They were no longer simple herders and farmers but a nation of emerging wealth and power. David wanted to establish for the Ark of the Covenant a permanent home, "exceeding magnificent, of fame and of glory throughout all lands" (1 Chron. 22:5). He made plans and gathered materials, but he died before the work could begin. Accord-

Solomon combined the attributes of tyrant and merchant prince. Revenues poured in from taxes on foreign caravans, from shipping and transport, and from flourishing trade with Phoenicia, Asia Minor, and Arabia. Solomon was, in fact, the chief horse trader of the ancient world. Although historians of subsequent eras came to consider Solomon's reign a sort of golden age, the Jews were still less technologically advanced than their neighbors. Therefore, when Solomon set about building the temple his father had planned, he commissioned architects, craftsmen, masons, and carpenters from his ally, the Phoenician King Hiram of Tyre. He drafted his own subjects for the unskilled labor.

A flight of steps led up to the temple façade, which was adorned with two ornate bronze columns thirty feet high. Between the columns, massive double doors of cedar opened onto a small porch set with lanterns. More steps led up to the main hall or sanctuary, where a host of daily rituals were performed, and a final flight of stairs led to a small, unlit cube-shaped chamber, the holy of holies. This chamber, a perfect replica in stone and wood of the original Tabernacle, was so sacred that the high priest could enter it only once a year. Here, the Ark of the Covenant was preserved.

The temple was not lofty, although its 50-foot-high roof topped with golden spikes may still have made it the tallest building in the land. Neither was it particularly large, being only 33 feet wide (not counting the storerooms that lined three sides) and 115 feet long. Its modest dimensions and simple façade of white limestone gave little hint of the magnificence within. The floors were made of cypress and the walls were of the cedar of Lebanon, inlaid with gold patterns of palm trees, vines, and flowers. Gold was everywhere, glinting from tables, candlesticks, and even from the nails in the floors and walls. The ark was guarded by two huge cherubim (not angels, in the modern

until, in 538 B.C., the Babylonians were themselves conquered.

The new victor, King Cyrus the Great of Persia, gave the exiled Jews permission to return home. There, spurred on by the prophet Haggai and funded by Cyrus, they began the enormous task of rebuilding their temple. While similar to Solomon's temple in structure, the new building was "as nothing" compared to its predecessor. The holy of holies was simply a dark, empty room, and a stone slab signified the absence of the ark. At the dedication in 515 B.C., while the young re-

joiced, the old wept, remembering the richly majestic shrine of earlier times.

Modest though it was, the Second Temple endured for five hundred years. Then, in 20 B.C., Herod the Great, King of Judea, undertook to raise the temple to new heights of splendor. Judea was, at that time, a Roman dominion, and when Herod rebuilt the temple, he employed the prevailing Hellenistic-Roman style. Ten thousand men worked for ten years to carry out his grandiose plans. The temple was embellished with nine gold- and silver-covered gates, a magnificent central

Far left, a nineteenth-century engraving showing the interior of the Dome of the Rock. This Old City mosque is named after the rock around which it was built. The rock is said to have been the main sacrificial altar of the ancient Temple of Jerusalem. Left, the Mosque of Aqsa which, like the Dome of the Rock, is located in the Haram esh Sharif. Below, a view from the Dome of the Rock.

meaning of the word, but lionlike creatures with wings and human faces), carved of olive wood and overlaid with gold.

This splendid temple lasted for about four hundred years. Then, in 587 B.C., the Babylonian King Nebuchadnezzar conquered what was left of Solomon's kingdom and pillaged the temple of its treasures. He apparently never found the Ark of the Covenant, which had been so well hidden by the prophet Jeremiah that, to this day, it has never been discovered. On the ninth day of the month of Ab (November), a date still commemorated by Jews, Nebuchadnezzar burned the Temple of Jerusalem to the ground. Thousands were deported from Jerusalem to Babylon, where they remained almost fifty years

gate of Corinthian bronze, and four courtyards (the largest, open to non-Jews, covered thirty-five acres) surrounded by a colonnaded walkway a mile long. Such magnificence of scale made Herod's temple one of the most striking buildings in the Roman Near East.

Its glory, however, was short-lived. The temple was still being improved in A.D. 67, when the Jews rebelled against Rome. After a three-year siege, Titus, who later succeeded his father as emperor of Rome, captured Jerusalem, and once more the temple was pillaged, burned, and razed to the ground—again on the ninth of Ab. Only that section of the retaining wall now called the Wailing Wall ultimately escaped destruction.

The Roman-Jewish war was one of the bloodiest the ancient world had ever seen. Afterward, the Jews were denied permission to build a fourth temple—a decree which led directly to the desperate attempt of Simon Bar Kokhba, a self-proclaimed messiah of legendary strength and bravery, to throw off the Roman yoke. But three years later in A.D. 135, the Romans were again victorious. Judea was reduced to the wasteland it was to remain for generations. Jerusalem was, for the most part, leveled and rebuilt as a Roman military colony, from which, except on the ninth of Ab, Jews were prohibited from entering on pain of crucifixion.

The Jews did not re-enter Jerusalem until 637, when the Moslems under Caliph Omar conquered the city and invited them to return. In an age of intense bigotry, the Moslems were surprisingly tolerant, and for a time all went well. Worshipers prayed freely at the Wailing Wall and even constructed a synagogue nearby. But soon religious harmony proved as elusive as it seems today. The Moslems, too, claimed Jerusalem as a holy city and the Wailing Wall an especially sacred spot. There, according to tradition, the angel Gabriel had tethered Mohammed's winged mare, Buraq, during the Prophet's Night Journey to Heaven. On the site of the Second Temple of Jerusalem, the Moslems constructed some of the city's most beautiful buildings—the Dome of the Rock, the Mosque of Aqsa, the Dome of the Chain—and enclosed them with a wall that incorporated the Wailing Wall itself.

Throughout the rest of Jerusalem's history—it has been the domain of Crusaders, Egyptians, Turks, and the British—the memory of the temple has never lost its hold on the scattered Jewish people. Even today, Orthodox Jews pray daily that the temple may be rebuilt. Its destruction is symbolically recalled at every Jewish wedding, when the groom crushes a glass under his heel.

Since the Six-Day War of 1967, the Wailing Wall, with the rest of the Old City of Jerusalem, has been once more in the possession of the Jewish people. After nineteen hundred years, the Jews have regained the Promised Land, and today, the stones of the Second Temple are as charged with Jewish faith and pride as when they were erected to the glory of Yahweh three thousand years ago.

Medina of Marrakesh

Morocco

Known as the "Capital of the South," Marrakesh has long been the meeting place of Mediterranean Islam and the Berber culture of the Atlas Mountains and the Sahara. Although it was founded as a military encampment, the true lifeblood of the city has always been commerce, and the crowded open-air market of the Djemaa el-Fna (preceding page), near the twelfth-century Koutoubia mosque, has been the heart of the business district for at least eight centuries.

The winding streets of the medina (left) which surround the plaza are devoted to the souks (markets). The busiest streets (above right) are covered to shield market-goers from the noonday sun. The drab street garb of many pedestrians (right and far right) contrasts with the deeply colored clay buildings which give Marrakesh the nickname "red city."

The old city, known as the medina, *remains largely untouched by modernization. Merchants do business from outdoor stalls (left) or simply spread their wares on the ground (below). Street musicians (above) are a common sight, as entertainment is as much a part of the market as shopping. The narrow streets of this district (facing page) limit traffic to an occasional bicycle or mo-ped. Here, the pedestrian is still all powerful.*

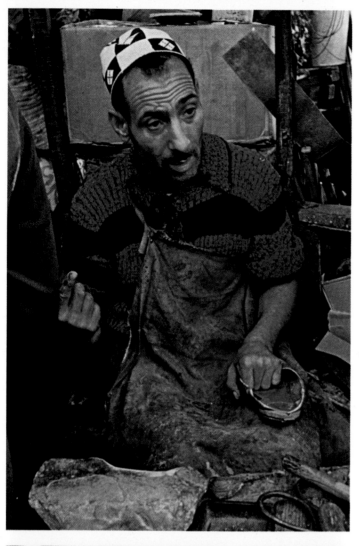

An astounding variety of goods is available in the Djemaa el-Fna and the surrounding souks. Cobblers (far left, above) fashion shoes and sandals to order. Far left, below, lathe operator makes wood pieces for the lattice behind him. Chickens (below left) are normally sold live or killed on the spot to insure freshness. Outdoor restaurants (above left) serve traditional Moroccan dishes, especially couscous, a crushed grain which is steamed and served with various meats and vegetables.

Above, a merchant displaying the ornate caftans that women wear in the privacy of their homes. Dates (right) are a staple food and customers may choose from among more than a dozen kinds and grades of quality. Below, produce and earthenware utensils, including tagine dishes with conical lids, used for cooking the ubiquitous spicy and fruit-flavored stews.

The most interesting parts of the market are the tanners' quarters (below), where skins are cured in huge vats of lime, and the colorful dyers' souk (above and facing page). Here, well-to-do merchants (left) oversee the dyeing of wool skeins which are then festooned overhead to dry.

The Bab Aguenau (following page), dating from A.D. 1150, is the finest gate into the old city.

Medina Of Marrakesh Morocco

The great plaza which marks the heart of the *medina*, or old city, of Marrakesh in Morocco is called the Djemaa el-Fna—the "meeting place of the dead." Hundreds of years ago, criminals were executed there, and the severed heads of traitors hung from its gates. Today, the character of the plaza is quite different. If anything, it is the rawness and abundance of life in this open-air marketplace which shock the first-time visitor. Here, among the rows of stalls where merchants and patrons haggle over the prices of produce, pottery, and souvenir caftans, the wandering tourist soon comes upon a row of outdoor barbershops where customers may combine a haircut with a quick tooth extraction or a blood-letting treatment, all performed in full view of passers-by. Scribes seated in the midst of the jostling crowds write letters and poems for the illiterate. Vendors display vials of fox saliva, sold as love charms, and pieces of jackal liver, guaranteed to keep the sleepy awake. An enterprising snake charmer solicits business by waving a hissing cobra in the face of a startled American tourist. And, of course, beggars of all descriptions, child and adult, healthy and deformed, converge on the newcomer demanding alms.

Many who initially find this scene daunting soon succumb to the fascination of watching the activity in this crowded market, which is as vital today as it was when Marrakesh first grew up around an ancient crossroads of North African caravan routes. Before the French occupation, similar though smaller market squares existed in other Moroccan cities. Fortunately, Marrakesh's *medina* escaped the modernization which destroyed so many of its counterparts. A persistent though undocumented story gives credit for its survival to Eleanor Roosevelt. At the Casablanca Conference during World War II, she is said to have expressed to Sultan Mohammed V her desire to revisit the square which she remembered from childhood travels. Whether or not this conversation was the deciding factor, the Djemaa el-Fna was preserved and has become the traditional site of Morocco's annual national folk festival.

During the twentieth century many foreigners have been drawn to exotic Marrakesh. The city has been a favorite winter spa of such celebrated Europeans as Winston Churchill. Later, plentiful hashish and cheap living made it a center of international hippiedom. Today, middle-class vacationers can view the hubbub of the market from the comfort of a resort hotel next door. Marrakesh has absorbed this influx of outsiders without harming its essential character. Foreigners blend into the crowds which already include descendants of Arabs from the Middle East, Berber tribesmen from the Atlas Mountains, and black Africans from Senegal and beyond. Even the products of Western

Above right, a Ptolemaic map from the Catalan Atlas (1375), now in the British Museum. The Berbers of southern Morocco adopted Islam at this time but remained a military power. One tribe, the Tuareg (right), continues to adhere to pre-Moslem customs, including the custom of men wearing veils.

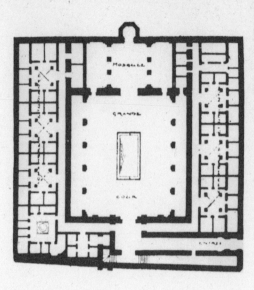

Left, the characteristic Islamic horseshoe arches of an aisle in the twelfth-century Koutoubia mosque. Right, plan of the madrasa of ibn-Yusuf, built in 1570 for the study of the Koran. Below, the interior of the madrasa.

industry are often displayed in uniquely Moroccan ways. A merchant may do a thriving business in used Wesson Oil cans, and a whole street of *souks* (markets) which open off the main square is peopled by craftsmen who fashion baskets, water jugs, and sandals from worn tires.

For all who gather there, the Djemaa el-Fna is a place of entertainment as well as commerce. The elite performers are the acrobats, traditionally natives of the nearby village of Amizmiz. Boy dancers of the Chleuh tribe, dressed as women, are another main attraction. Around the performers, wandering musicians, snake charmers, and operators of gambling games compete for attention. Perhaps the most popular entertainers of all, however, are the storytellers. In a society that is still largely illiterate, the balladeers retain their importance as chroniclers of legend and history, as well as bearers of the latest news. In fact, during the struggle against colonialism, the storytellers were banned and the Djemaa el-Fna was closed to prevent the spread of subversive ideas. Today, the storytellers flourish once more

and regale their audiences with tales and ballads that hark back to the heroic Almoravid dynasty which founded Marrakesh in the year A.D. 1062.

The ancestors of the Almoravids were the Sanhaja Berbers. This warlike tribe had adopted Islam after the Arab conquest of the north in the eighth century, although they did not allow the new religion to interfere with ancient traditions that included drinking alcohol and permitting their women to go unveiled; strangely enough, the men kept their faces covered. Then, in about 1050, their emir, Yahya ibn-Ibrahim, undertook a pilgrimage to Mecca and returned full of zeal for orthodoxy. Unenthusiastic about their leader's demands for piety, the Sanhaja banished him and his chief follower, a

holy man named Abdallah ibn-Yasin. Both men retreated to a *ribat*, or fortified monastery, and gathered a corps of disaffected warriors who subjected themselves to a harsh regimen of prayer reinforced by physical punishment. These highly disciplined soldiers became the nucleus of the Almoravids, a confederation of tribal armies which overran the Sahara and eventually challenged Arab predominance on the shores of the Mediterranean and in Andalusian Spain.

The Almoravids were empire builders, and in 1062, their leader, Yusuf ibn-Tashfin, chose to create a new city, conveniently situated between the original home of his people in the Sahara and the northern territories, where they had strong military ambitions.

The acquisition of an empire soon diluted the religious fervor of the Almoravids. Less than a century later, they were challenged by yet another Berber pilgrim, Mohammed ibn-Tumart, who had returned from Mecca preaching a complex doctrine of the unity of the godhead, from which his followers became known as *al-muhadin* (unitarians). Once again, a small sect of the faithful soon grew into a military force to be reckoned with. In 1147, the last Almoravid monarch was killed in battle at Marrakesh, and the city fell to an Almohad general, Abd al-Mumin.

Under the Almohads, Marrakesh grew from a military outpost into the first city of southern Morocco, and the landmarks which still remain its major architectural features were constructed. Abd al-Mumin began by enlarging and improving the red clay walls which, along with the color of the surrounding countryside, have given Marrakesh its age-old nickname of the "red city." Otherwise, the new masters of the land obliterated all reminders of their predecessors. The Almoravid palace of Dar el-Ajar was demolished, and in its place rose an imposing mosque, the Koutoubia. The mosque's 226-foot minaret was completed in the late twelfth century, after the dedication of the mosque itself in 1158. This graceful tower has often been copied, notably in the famous Giralda of Seville and the Hassan Tower in Rabat, yet it remains the pre-eminent symbol of Marrakesh. Koutoubia means "mosque of the books," and according to one six-teenth-century historian, Leo Africanus, the name recalls the booksellers' *souk* which stood near its site. Others claim that the designation refers to the library found in the mosque itself. In any case, the Dje-maa el-Fna, which lies in the shadow of the Koutoubia, was already established as the center of a thriving marketplace under the Almohads.

The third monarch of this dynasty, Yaqub al-Mansur, known as the Black Sultan because of his descent from an African slave girl, was an indefatigable builder and a strong administrator. His major contribution to the city was the Casbah—a walled enclave containing twelve separate palaces, a large mosque,

offices, and ornamental gardens. The term casbah, meaning citadel, is often applied to the entire precolonial sectors of North African cities. In Marrakesh, however, the name Casbah usually refers to the quarter of the *medina* established by the Black Sultan and the Koutoubia mosque, which still stands on the site.

To provide a suitably grand entrance to his palace enclave, Yaqub al-Mansur cut a large opening in the city ramparts and constructed a splendid gate of blue *gueliz* stone, carved in low relief and fitted with a series of splayed arches. This was the Bab Aguenau, or Gate of the Guineans, still

the most celebrated and elaborate of all the entrances to the old city.

Like the humbler parts of the *medina*, the Casbah was continually torn down and rebuilt as successive dynasties followed the Almohad custom of leaving little of the work of their forebears intact. Because of this tradition, the memory of one of the great periods in Marrakesh's history, that of Saadi rule between 1524 and 1688, was almost obliterated. A Saadi sultan, Ahmad al-Mansur, conquered Timbuktu in 1591, and the booty of gold, slaves, salt, and ivory made Marrakesh, for the first

In 1844, French troops defeated Moroccan allies of the emir of Algiers at the Battle of Isly (top), beginning the process of colonization which was completed shortly after the death of Sultan Moulay Abd al-Aziz (above) in 1908. Mohammed V (left) presided over the liberation of Morocco in 1956.

time, a rich city as well as a proud one. Yet, for centuries, the only visible symbol of this era was the Badi Palace, a formerly magnificent structure that had been reduced to ruins by a seventeenth-century sultan, Moulay Ismail.

It was not until 1917, when the French had been in control of Morocco for five years, that a group of laborers broke through a wall in the Casbah's great mosque and discovered the treasures of the Saadians. Here, hidden from history since it had been walled up by Moulay Ismail, was the mausoleum of the Saadi rulers. This series of tombs, fitted with

Djemaa el-Fna are still divided into quarters of different groups of artisans, who practice their crafts much as their ancestors did centuries ago. There are *souks* for leather workers, for copper and silver engravers, and for the tanners, who cure skins according to an old formula which involves long soaking in a lime bath, followed by successive treatments with crushed bark, pigeon dung, and the pulp of mashed dates and figs. For jewelry, one goes to the Mellah, or Jewish quarter, where a large population of Orthodox Jews has lived since 1558. Perhaps the most interesting sight in the *souks*, how-

ever, is the dyers' quarter, where colorful skeins of freshly dyed wool are hung overhead to dry.

By late afternoon, the crowd begins to disperse from the Djemaa el-Fna. As a hard day of bargaining draws to a close, businessmen wearing turbans and the traditional long, flowing robes called *djellabas* retreat to a sidewalk cafe for mint tea. They watch jugglers, musicians, monkey trainers, and often one or two miracle workers, members of Moslem religious fraternities who, for a few coins, will demonstrate their ability to drink boiling water or walk barefoot over shards of glass. The outdoor restaurants in the center of the square begin their business, and vendors appear with cart loads of hot soup, roasted snails, or cooling drinks, depending on the season. Illuminated by strings of dim light bulbs, the plaza takes on an inviting glow, and often, the same tourists who were so dazed by the spectacle of the morning are seen strolling peacefully or joining the amazed audiences to watch the performers.

A true understanding of life of the *medina* would require years of study, but in Marrakesh even casual visitors find themselves participating in it through the activity of the market. For the Djemaa el-Fna is not merely a tourist attraction but a meeting place of the centuries.

columns of marble from Carrara in Italy, with enameled tiles and intricate cedar woodcarvings, is a testament to the city's position as a cultural crossroads. The tombs reflect the influence of the Italian Renaissance, imposed upon an architectural style that had its roots in Hispano-Moorish design under the Almohads and was refined and elaborated under later dynasties.

The discovery of the Saadi tombs was a reminder of the imperial and artistic history of Marrakesh, but its greatest heritage—commerce—had never been lost. Even the building of the modern French sector outside the *medina* walls did not destroy the market center. The ancient, twisting streets which radiate from the

Among the unusual entertainments presented in the marketplace of Marrakesh are a duel with staves (above) and a singer who accompanies himself on an ancient stringed instrument, the gimbrel (right).

The Bazaar of Damascus

Syria

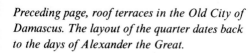

Preceding page, roof terraces in the Old City of Damascus. The layout of the quarter dates back to the days of Alexander the Great.

Left, a Corinthian capital on one of the columns of the Great Mosque, which stands on the site of several previous shrines: an Aramaean shrine to the god Hadad, a temple to Jupiter, and a Christian church dedicated to Saint John the Baptist.

Below left, the arcade of the west gallery of the mosque.

Right, mosaics over the entrance of the mosque seen from the inside of the vestibule.

Below right, the courtyard of the mosque. Polychrome mosaic work—in places rather fragmentary—covers the arcades of the galleries around three sides of the courtyard.

In 1749, Assad Pasha al-Azm, governor of Damascus, built a beautiful palace in the city as his personal residence. Located close to the Great Mosque, the palace preserves the splendor of bygone ages.

Left, below, and facing page, the patio, with its low reflecting pool in the center. Pools and fountains relieve the arid desert heat and are a recurrent feature of Moslem palaces.

The great iwan of the courtyard (center left) is a place of refuge from the sun.

The palace is now a folk museum (below left) and houses a collection of crafts.

Far left, the west entrance to the Great Mosque. Beside it are two of the remaining columns of the Roman Temple of Jupiter, built in the third century B.C. The temple was built on the site of an Aramaean shrine dedicated to the god Hadad. Left, an alley in the residential district of al-Kaimariye in the Old City of Damascus, where craftsmen work with wood. Crafts are still practiced in the residential districts, while commerce predominates in the souks. Buildings overhang the alley, thus shading it from the blazing sun. Below left, stones of the Old City wall.

Right, Arabic writing in bas-relief on a pillar of the north entrance colonnade of the Great Mosque. Below, two views of the alleyways in the al-Kaimariye.

Left, top row, stalls in the al-Hamidiya souk selling metal ware, glass, and slippers. The metal ware is damascened, a term applied to a technique whereby fine threads of gold or silver are inlaid in articles of metal, leather, or cloth. The technique spread from Damascus to Spain and the Far East. Below left, the main street of the souks of Damascus. The street is completely covered with sheets of corrugated iron borne on metal arches. It is strictly a pedestrian precinct and is crowded with shops of every kind. Merchants selling cloth, fancy goods, and jewelry vie for the customer's attention. Authentic works of art, no longer available in the souks, can only be found in antique shops or in museums. Right and below right, stalls in the souk of al-Hamidiya.

Following page, the Mosque of the Madrasa al-Suleimaniya, built in the Byzantine style in 1553 for Suleiman the Magnificent.

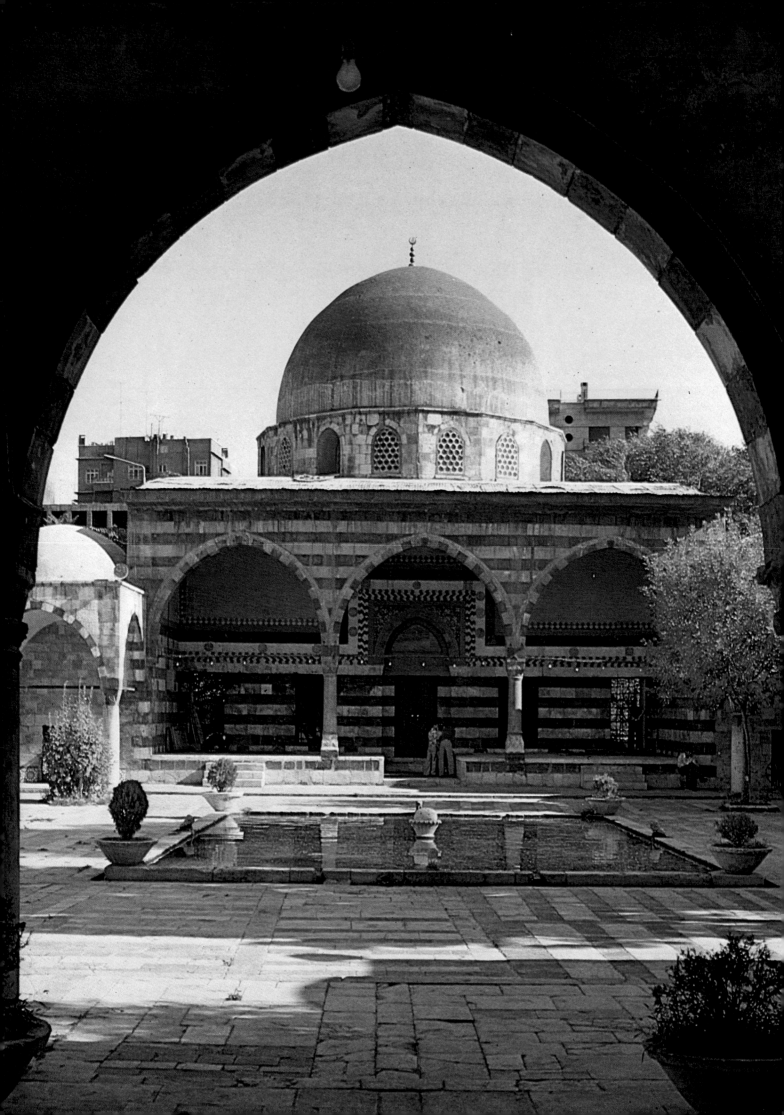

The Bazaar of Damascus Syria

The Syrian capital of Damascus is thought to be the oldest continuously inhabited city in the world. According to tradition, it was founded by a descendant of Noah's son, Shem. The earliest historical reference to the city is found in Egyptian hieroglyphic tablets, which list it as one of the cities conquered by Thutmose III during the fifteenth century B.C. Since that time, Persian, Alexandrian, Roman, Byzantine, and Arabic empires have all claimed the city at various times throughout the centuries.

From across the wastes of the Syrian Desert, Damascus is an extraordinary sight. Its nearly three hundred minarets stand tall against the sky, justifying its description as the "city of many pillars." Equally impressive are the city's gardens, which each spring are ablaze with the blossoms of peach trees and the distinctive orange-red of pomegranate flowers. Indeed, Moslem tradition regards the Ghuta oasis, on which Damascus was founded, as an earthly paradise.

The city reached its height as the capital of the Islamic empire under the Umayyad dynasty (A.D. 660–750). Some of its inhabitants still wear the costume that dates from those days—baggy trousers, turban, and pointed red shoes. Sometimes a solitary veiled woman appears on the street or a wealthy citizen, dressed in white silk, rides by with a long dagger in his belt. Donkeys trot through the city's alleys and markets; Kurdish shepherds, dressed in capes of checked felt, drive their flocks to market. Then there are the Bedouins on their spirited horses and, occasionally, the majestic spectacle of a caravan of dromedaries laden with grain.

Though Damascus contains several splendid buildings, including the Great Mosque, a Roman citadel, and the eighteenth-century palace of Assad Pasha al-Azm, it has always been best known as a center of trade. As far back as the Middle Ages, the city was receiving merchants from nearly every part of the known world.

The visitor entering the ancient central quarter, or Old City, of Damascus finds himself in the teeming *souks,* or covered

markets. This type of market is said to be as old as the East. The *souks* originally arose under the direction of the various craft guilds, which assigned goods to different sections of the market according to type. Thus, the supervisor of each guild was able to keep an eye on business and regulate the quality of the items being sold. Though modern influences pervade this ancient marketplace, bringing in goods aimed at the tourist trade, the ancient flavor of Damascus remains.

The *souk* of al-Arwam lies near the heart of the city, southeast of the old Marjah Square. Here, in the ancient Jewish quarter, is a series of markets, each with its own specialty: the al-Hamir *souk,* with its donkey sellers, and the as-Surudschige, or

Above right, the courtyard of the Great Mosque, as it appeared early in this century. In the center is the fountain of purification, where the faithful wash before entering the mosque. Right, a miniature showing a caravan of Arab merchants, from an eleventh-century manuscript. Even after losing its status as the Umayyad capital in A.D. 750, Damascus continued to be a lively center of trade.

In the early sixteenth century, the Ottoman Sultan Selim I defeated the last of the Abbasid caliphs and entered Damascus in triumph to reign over Egypt and Syria. Below, his coronation.

Right, the viceroy of Egypt, Mehemet Ali, who fought the sultan of Constantinople for possession of Syria. His campaign ended in 1840, when Syria was once again annexed by the Ottoman Empire. Above, an eighteenth-century painting of Tamerlane the Tartar, who conquered Damascus in 1399.

chair-seller's *souk*. In the *souk* of an-Nahhasin, coppersmiths offer magnificent copper trays, called *kuni,* mounted on wooden tripods. The Ali Pasha *souk* overflows with the renowned fruit of Damascus: dried peaches, dates, apricots, bunches of the plump grapes that were especially prized in medieval Constantinople, and purple plums famed throughout the eastern Mediterranean.

These *souks* lie close to the moats of the Citadel, a fortress that dates from the Roman occupation in the first century B.C. The Citadel rests on the remains of a Roman encampment, relics of which are still visible within its walls. The fortress stretches along the natural moat of the

Barada, the river that feeds the oasis of Ghuta. With its twelve square towers, the Citadel owes its present appearance to Malik al-Adil, the brother of the great Sultan Saladin, who in the early years of the thirteenth century, equipped it for siege warfare. Centuries later, it is still kept in a state of readiness.

The eastern gate of the Citadel, which was decorated in the thirteenth century with sumptuous honeycomb work, leads into the al-Hamidiya *souk.* Here is another maze of shops, newer than those in the al-Arwam. The merchants offer pipes, clothing, religious articles, and weapons, all at moderate prices. Old daggers and swords are often touted as examples of the

fabled blades of Damascus steel, which were greatly prized throughout the ancient and medieval world. These weapons, with intricate tracery on their blades, date at least from the time of Diocletian (ca. A.D. 290). History records that, when Tamerlane, the Tartar conqueror, entered Damascus in 1399, the sword makers, along with certain other artisans, were spared in the subsequent blood bath. But Tamerlane then carried them off to his own capital of Samarkand, thus arresting the great tradition of sword making in Damascus. For this reason, it is advisable to suspect the authority of the vendors who extol the authenticity of the blades that are sold today in the al-Hamidiya.

Close by the antique sellers are the merchants who sell ceramics and glassware. In these arts, Damascus has excelled since before the birth of Christ. Syrian craftsmen were among the most skillful pupils of the Persian masters of the art of ceramics. In the ninth and tenth centuries, Islam forbade the representation of the human figure, so potters embellished their work with plant and animal motifs, as well as with various inscriptions in stylized Arabic calligraphy.

The ancient Damascenes were also skilled as glassmakers. Pliny, the first-century Roman historian, considered the Syrian (now Lebanese) towns of Tyre and Sidon the principal glass-producing centers of his world, referring to Sidon as *"Sido artifex vitri"* ("Sidon, skilled in glassware"). Damascus glass was popular throughout the Middle East from the thirteenth to the fifteenth centuries, the most famous pieces being the highly decorated mosque lamps. Cups, small vials, and lamps still survive, their delicate forms enriched by an opalescent patina. Though of inferior quality, glassware is still produced in Damascus, decorated in traditional fashion with intricate floral and geometric motifs.

Tanners now occupy the *khan* (exchange for foreign traders) al-Harir. Their craft still uses the ancient techniques that made their leather work famous throughout Syria, Italy, and Moslem Spain. Decorated silk and carpets are sold in the *khan* of Suleiman Pasha. In medieval Europe, silk goods from Syria were much in demand, and the Crusaders used the cloth for wrapping sacred relics. Damask was the name given to the silk brocaded with flowers, plants, birds, and other animals, often interwoven with gold and silver threads. Syrian carpet weavers combined the Egyptian style, which dates at least from the time of the Pharaohs, with that of the Persians, whose carpets have always been highly esteemed.

Near the silk and carpet market stand a few massive Corinthian columns supporting fragments of an architrave. This ruin is all that remains of the Temple of Jupiter,

Left, a nineteenth-century engraving showing the interior of a bazaar in Damascus. A traditional local craft is the manufacture of worked silks, called damask after the name of the city.

Below, an old view of Damascus, dominated by the Great Mosque.

built in the third century B.C., during the Roman occupation. Over three millenniums this site has been sanctified by a succession of temples built by the various religious groups that predominated in Damascus. The Roman columns stand on the ruins of a shrine to the god Hadad, erected by the Aramaeans, a people who inhabited Syria around 1200 B.C. Toward the end of the fourth century, Damascus was an important military outpost of the Byzantine Empire. Christianity became the dominant religion and the Temple of Jupiter was turned into a cathedral dedicated to Saint John the Baptist. Then in A.D. 635, when the Arabs conquered the city, the eastern half of the church was used for Moslem worship. Seventy years

later, the Umayyad Caliph al-Walid I took possession of the entire sanctuary and rebuilt it as a mosque.

The Great Mosque is still believed to house a precious Christian relic—the head of Saint John. The structure is built on the cruciform Byzantine plan. The Byzantine influence is doubtless attributable to the twelve hundred Byzantine craftsmen who were sent by the emperor of the Holy Roman Empire to assist with the construction. Characteristically, the interior consists of an open space surrounded on three sides by a portico and a covered space of three long naves that are crossed in the middle by a perpendicular nave.

It is difficult to determine how much of the earlier Christian structure al-Walid preserved. The two southern minarets of the mosque are built over the towers of the church, while the northern one is the work either of al-Walid or another of the Umayyad rulers, who were the first in all Islam to build minarets.

In the south wall of the Great Mosque is the *mihrab,* a niche that directs worshipers toward Mecca. Though the *mihrab* had traditionally been used in palace architecture, it is thought that al-Walid was the first to build one in a mosque. The caliph also had the walls and floor of the mosque covered with marble and with magnificent mosaics, incorporating complex abstract

patterns and inscriptions. Six hundred golden lamps hung from the ceiling.

The mosque has undergone considerable damage since its days of Umayyad glory. One caliph covered over the mosaics, and they were not rediscovered until 1928. In 1069, the mosque was damaged by fire, and in the fifteenth century, it was ravaged by conquerors. In 1893, it was again damaged by fire, and the existing marble work dates from this period. But despite these disasters, the mosque retains much of its original plan and is still a structure of singular beauty.

One of the more brilliant periods of Syrian history was during the reign of the Sultan Saladin (1171–1193). Damascus still bears the imprint of his cultural achievements. Saladin is best known in the West for his valiant campaigns against the Crusaders. An enlightened and munificent ruler, he considered education the most powerful political weapon. Under his rule, Damascus became a city of schools. Ibn-Jubayr, an Andalusian traveler who reached the city in 1184, recorded the existence of twenty *madrasas,* or Koran schools, numerous dervish monasteries, and two free hospitals—all of which were constructed under Saladin's direction. These buildings laid the foundation for the great flowering of classical Islamic architecture.

It is the *souks,* even more than the ancient buildings, that preserve the exotic, cosmopolitan spirit of Damascus. Despite the gradual introduction of modern goods and customs, they remain essentially as they have been for centuries. In the Old City, the al-Bazuriye *souk* sells candied apricots and, nearby, the air is sweet with the fragrances of violets and rosewater from the perfume *souk* of al-Attarin.

Just off the Via Recta—named in Acts of the Apostles, "the street which is called straight"—is the *souk* of Midhat Pasha. Here, the wood-turners, with their characteristic foot-driven lathes, make inlaid supports for *kuni,* the copper trays sold in the an-Nahhasin *souk.* And throughout the market, thousands of craftsmen are hammering copper, carving wood, and beating leather, with tools that have scarcely changed in a thousand years.

Another famous craft of Damascus is the celebrated Damascene blades. Above, workmen sharpening swords in the Old City.

Right, a view of the center of Damascus, showing Marjah Square. In the center is the column of Ta Mecqua.

The Kaaba at Mecca

Saudi Arabia

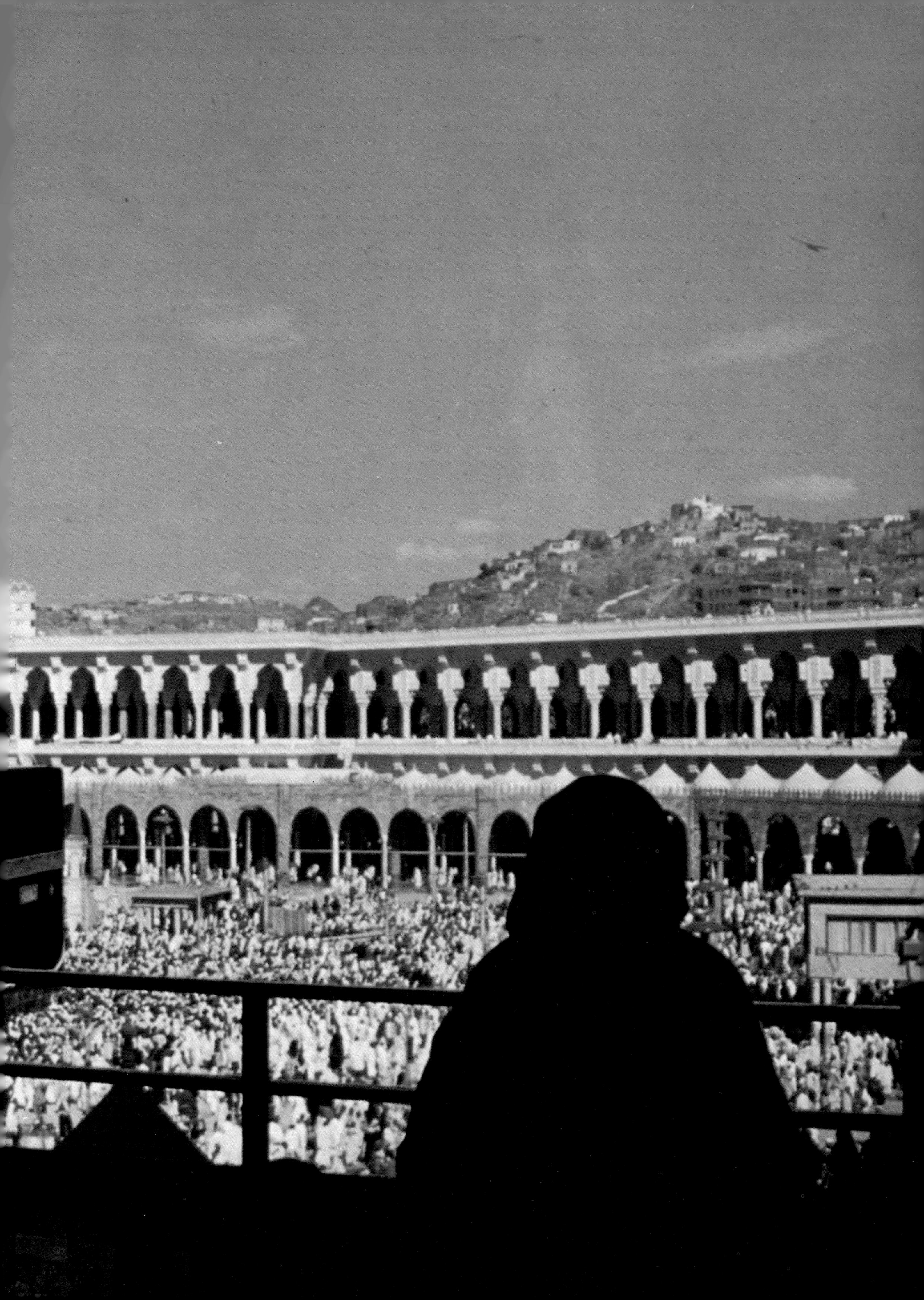

Preceding page, a view of the courtyard in Mecca where the Kaaba stands, a religious shrine that is even older than Islam. Legends trace the first temple on this site back to Adam. Even the custom of draping this boxlike stone structure in black cloth predates the birth of the Prophet Mohammed. The columns of the surrounding portico are made of marble.

Pilgrims converge on the city in cars and buses and on foot (above and left).

Above right, two views of pilgrims at prayer in an encampment on the way to Mecca. In accordance with Islamic law, they have removed their shoes to pray. Right, the Black Stone in its silver mounting. Such stones, of meteoric origin, were often regarded as sacred in ancient times.

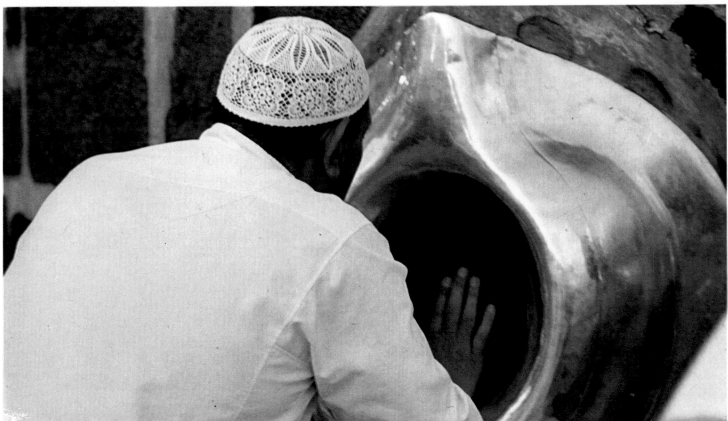

The courtyard of the Kaaba functions as an open-air temple. Only the shrine itself is roofed, and in ancient times even this structure stood open to the sky. The first roof was constructed in the time of Mohammed and was such a novelty in the Arabian Desert that roof beams had to be salvaged from a ship wrecked on the coast of the Red Sea.

Left and below, the annual cleaning of the Kaaba. This is the only time of the year when the shrine is opened and the black cloth is replaced.

Perhaps the most impressive moment of all is the evening prayer (facing page) when thousands recite with the imam (prayer leader) the words, "Allah is almighty."

The courtyard becomes a sea of humanity when the faithful crowd together to perform their ritual obeisances (following page). For many, this moment represents the culmination of a lengthy journey, often thousands of miles long. Those gathered here are not, however, on the yearly pilgrimage, for they are not dressed in the ritual garb of pilgrims.

Above left, armed Arab Bedouins in traditional garb. Left, male pilgrims to Mecca wearing the ihram, a garment consisting of two pieces of white cloth, one draped around the waist and the other thrown over the shoulder and wrapped around the chest. The garment eliminates distinctions of national origin and class and sets the pilgrims apart from the residents of Mecca.

Mecca is the cradle of Islamic thought. The imams of Mecca (above) are guardians of an ancient tradition, and their interpretations of the law and doctrine carry considerable authority. Moslems (above right) gather at a pilgrim station en route to Medina.

Right, the tomb of Mohammed in Medina, some two hundred miles north of Mecca. It was the Prophet himself who cleansed the Kaaba of idols and established the hadj, or pilgrimage, as one of the major obligations of the Moslem religion.

Following page, the Kaaba, viewed through a grating in the wall of the outer portico. This portico is a product of the last substantial renovation of this site, completed during the era of Turkish domination. Though rebuilt many times, the Kaaba is considered a faithful reproduction of the temples of Adam and Abraham.

The Kaaba at Mecca Saudi Arabia

Some monuments are prized for their beauty, others for their importance in the life of a people. The Kaaba, the sanctuary at Mecca, belongs to the second category. The Kaaba is considered by Moslems to be the most sacred spot on earth, so sacred that non-Moslems are forbidden to set eyes on it. Only a few Christians—perhaps the most famous being the nineteenth-century English explorer, Sir Richard Burton—have successfully violated this prohibition. The accounts of these daring travelers tend to confirm the wisdom of excluding nonbelievers, for the glories of the Kaaba cannot be measured by the aesthetic standards of the infidel.

The word *kaaba* in Arabic means, literally, a "cube." The Kaaba at Mecca is not a perfectly geometric cube, but the name aptly describes this plain, boxlike structure of mortared stone. Inside, the Kaaba is empty except for three pillars which support the roof and hundreds of gold and silver lamps hanging from the ceiling. Outside the sanctuary, worshipers focus their attention on the sacred Black Stone, which is mounted in silver at the eastern corner of the Kaaba. This relic, most likely a meteorite, is said by the sages to symbolize the human soul shining under the throne of God, although it was long ago worn dull under the hands and lips of countless pilgrims.

One of the most striking features of the Kaaba, although perhaps more strange than beautiful, is the immense black cloth in which the entire building is swathed. Woven into the fabric in gold thread is the Moslem credo, "There is no God but Allah and Mohammed is his Prophet."

Above, a miniature from a manuscript of 1314 depicting Mohammed replacing the Black Stone at the completion of a restoration of the Kaaba.

Far right, Adam and Eve in an Islamic painting of the early seventeenth century. Islam holds the entire Old Testament sacred and reveres its prophets as predecessors of Mohammed.

Right, a plan of the Kaaba's enclosure, taken from the "Book of Origins," a sixteenth-century Arab manuscript.

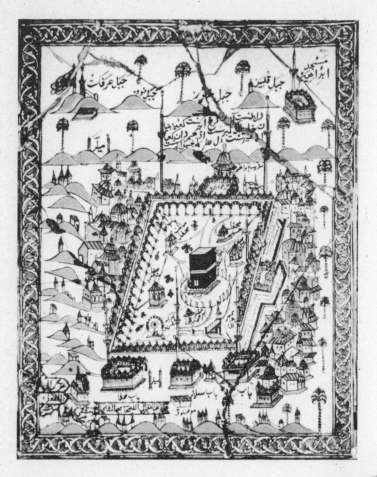

Every day, devout Moslems bow five times toward this unprepossessing monument, and for fourteen centuries, believers of all social classes have traveled thousands of miles and faced untold hardships for the privilege of praying outside its walls.

Spiritually and historically, the Kaaba is the center of Islam, but many centuries before the birth of the Prophet Mohammed, it was already venerated as the mythical point of origin of the Arab race. The early Arabs, whose name recalls their origins as a "people of the desert," worshiped hundreds of deities, although one god, Allah, has apparently always reigned supreme.

According to Arab legend, the Kaaba was the first temple to Allah and the original house of God, constructed by Adam himself. After being cast out from the presence of God, Adam wandered in despair until, in the bleak valleys of the Hejaz region of Arabia, he received a sign of forgiveness. Under a ruby canopy supported by four emerald columns shone a pearly stone so radiant that it illuminated the entire valley. Adam walked seven

times around this vision, establishing a tradition still followed by pilgrims today. He then gathered rocks from nearby Mount Hira to erect a wall around the site. This was the beginning of the Kaaba, which according to legend is the world's first work of architecture. The temple was also the first monument to be pillaged in favor of a later one when, upon Adam's death, the shining stone was removed to his tomb on Mount Qubais.

Tradition links the Kaaba with the other patriarch, Abraham, who discovered the foundations of Adam's temple, which had been destroyed by the Flood. He scrupulously reconstructed the original floor plan of the temple, an irregular quadrilateral whose four walls are 32, 22,

Above left, a nineteenth-century ceramic tile made in Syria showing the city of Mecca which surrounds the courtyard of the Kaaba.

Left, Abd al-Malik, a seventh-century military leader who extended the boundaries of Islam.

Above, Saladin, the sultan who wrenched Jerusalem from the Crusaders in 1187.

37, and 20 ells (a forty-five-inch measurement) long. This, indeed, is the shape of the Kaaba today. Abraham was assisted in his labor by his son, Ishmael, who did the heavy work, carrying boulders "as big as camels." Although he ventured deep into the surrounding hills, Ishmael could find no stone special enough to mark the corner where the ritual circumambulation of the shrine was to begin. One day Ishmael returned empty-handed from the search to discover that the pearly stone of Adam's vision had been miraculously transported from Mount Qubais to the eastern corner of the rebuilt temple. The Kaaba was now complete, and Abraham issued the call to worship which is still answered by pilgrims today.

Other than traditional accounts, few facts can be substantiated about the origin of the Kaaba. It is known, however, that the Kaaba was a long-established sanctuary during the ninth century B.C., when the Assyrian kings were fighting against the people of the desert. But over the centuries, the shrine that Abraham had built to the one God had become a house of idols. As many as 360 images of tribal deities were arranged along the Kaaba's walls, including representations of Abraham and Ishmael.

The concept of monotheism was not entirely lost in the Hejaz, but for hundreds of years it was preserved only by Hebrew tribes who settled among the Arabs, adopted their customs, and converted many of the desert people to Judaism. One influential convert was As'ad Abu Karib, a king of the Himyar dynasty which traced its lineage back to the queen of Sheba. Karib, who had come to Mecca for plunder, was inspired by a dream to "clothe" the Kaaba, first with a covering of palm leaves and, later, with striped cloth from Yemen. The custom is still honored today, although the covering is now a rich brocade manufactured in Egypt and replaced annually with great ceremony.

During the period of greatest Jewish influence, Christianity, too, reached Mecca and was assimilated into Arab polytheism. Pictures of the Madonna and Child were added to the Kaaba's pantheon, and Christian Arabs joined Jews and pagans in worship at the sanctuary.

By this time, the building attributed to Abraham had undergone several reconstructions, and the city of Mecca had grown up around the monument. Mecca was organized according to a rigid class system—its founder and his descendants lived around the Kaaba's courtyard. Allied tribes were settled around them in concentric circles. The lowliest classes—slaves, mercenaries, and foreigners—were relegated to the fringes of the city.

In A.D. 570, Mecca was invaded by an Ethiopian governor of southern Arabia who had vowed to convert the city to Christianity. It is said that, just as the governor was about to raze the Kaaba itself, his elephant suddenly knelt in front of the shrine and refused to advance. Fifty-five

Abd al-Muttalib, the grandfather of Mohammed, is said to have dug the well of Zamzam whose curative waters are drunk by pilgrims. The sixteenth-century manuscript illustration (left) shows him paying homage at the Kaaba.

Under Suleiman the Magnificent (below left), the Ottoman Empire stretched from the Balkans to Arabia. The last renovation of the Kaaba was planned during his reign.

Below, wealthy pilgrims arriving in Mecca on a litter carried by two camels.

days after this dramatic sign of God's protection, Mohammed, the future Prophet of Islam, was born.

Thirty-five years later, the citizens of Mecca rebuilt the Kaaba once again. When the renovation was nearly finished, the story is told of an argument that arose over who was to have the honor of replacing the shrine's sacred stone. It was finally agreed to let the next man who chanced to enter the courtyard make the decision. That man was Mohammed. He pacified the disputing tribesmen by placing the stone on a cloth and asking a representative of each faction to hold the corners while he lifted the stone into its niche.

At the time of Mohammed's fortuitous involvement with the Kaaba, he was simply a respectable local merchant. Within a few years, his position in the community had radically altered. A succession of revelations led Mohammed to believe that he had been chosen for a divine mission, and at the age of forty, he declared himself the Messenger of Allah. The Prophet initially inspired more hostility than support and was forced to flee his enemies in Mecca for the safety of Medina. In 630, he returned to his home city after an eight-year exile. His first act in Mecca was to pay the traditional homage at the Kaaba; the second

was to call for the keys to the sanctuary and remove the idols within, leaving only the images of Abraham, Jesus, and the Virgin.

Thus purified, the Kaaba became the spiritual center of the rapidly expanding Moslem empire. After Mohammed's death, his followers quarreled over who should succeed him, and in the ensuing civil war, stones from catapults were fired into the temple courtyard, cracking the Black Stone. The temple was soon divided into sections, each reserved for one of the numerous Islamic sects. One of these sects, the Karmathians, even succeeded in carrying off the Black Stone. Twenty-two years later, it was ransomed and returned to Mecca, but by then it had been broken into several pieces.

Despite these depredations, the Kaaba's spiritual significance continued to grow. Pilgrims, obeying the Prophet's exhortation to visit Mecca at least once in a lifetime, converged on the city from all parts of the Moslem world. To accommodate the crush of visitors, the Turkish rulers of Arabia began yet another reconstruction in 1612. Following plans drawn up decades earlier under the Sultan Suleiman the Magnificent, the portico of the courtyard

was enlarged to its present size of 537 by 550 feet. Marble columns replaced stone ones, and the portico's nineteen doors were made even more splendid.

The restoration of the Kaaba met with staunch resistance from the imams (religious leaders) of Mecca, who would rather have seen the temple collapse around the heads of the faithful than have the stones desecrated. This traditionalist attitude prevailed until the middle of the seventeenth century, when the existing structure was leveled by a flood and the sultan of Constantinople sent his own chamberlain to direct the rebuilding. The chamberlain, who must have feared for his head if the project did not go well, prayed for guidance while coordinating the work of architects from India, Constantinople, and other parts of the Islamic world.

All did go well, and today the Kaaba continues to receive pilgrims who reflect the racial, cultural, and linguistic diversity of the religion founded by Mohammed. Moslem pilgrims still kiss the Black Stone that had already been the object of devotion centuries before it was first touched by the Prophet himself. For, in the words of the Koran, the Kaaba is the "first temple of mankind."

This early nineteenth-century drawing, shows details of the Kaaba's setting as it was then. The black cloth that covers the temple is embroidered in gold with quotations from the Koran.

Machu Picchu

Peru

Untouched by the Spanish conquest, the terraced city of Machu Picchu preserves the glory of Incan civilization high on an Andean ridge. Preceding page, walled compounds (foreground) which once contained the dwellings of Incan clans. On top of the small conical hill beyond the compounds to the left is the sanctuary of the Intihuatána, "the place where the sun is tied." Its carved spiral form may have symbolized the sun god's course through the sky.

One of the grandest of the city's one hundred granite stairways leads to the quarters of the nobility (left).

Above and right, the semicircular tower facing away from the peak of Huayna Picchu (above left). Alongside the tower is the wall considered by its discoverer to be the most beautiful in America.

Dazzling processions of Incan worshipers once mounted the stairway from the Sacred Plaza to the top of Intihuatána hill (above left) to observe the winter solstice.

Peasants living on the outskirts of the city supplied it with food grown on extensive and laboriously constructed terraces (above). Right and left, peasant dwellings on the terraces. The thatched roofing has been reconstructed.

The corner of the nobles' quarters (above right) shows a combination of styles of Incan masonry—large rectangular blocks sitting on a jigsaw pattern of closely fitted, polygonal stones.

Although one end of the Main Temple in the Sacred Plaza (above left) has settled, the stones were originally placed with exacting precision. The huge altar is a granite monolith fourteen feet long and five feet high.

Far left, the Temple of the Three Windows. Left, one of the finest of the trapezoidal niches found in Incan homes, used as cupboards—or perhaps as repositories for the ancestral mummies. The edges of the granite blocks are gently rounded.

The semicircular tower (above right), very similar to the Temple of the Sun in Cuzco, was built around an outcropping of rock that probably had a sacred significance. Right, the main gate, seen from the inside. The stone ring above the lintel and the cylindrical stones set into the sides were used to secure a heavy log door.

Facing page, the view eastward through the central window of the remarkable three-windowed wall, looking out over the Urubamba gorge. The river is visible below the houses (right). Above, the Intihuatána, to which the priests "tied" the sun at the winter solstice to make it come back. The Spaniards broke off the upright part of these sacred stones wherever they found them; this intact one indicates that the conquerors never reached Machu Picchu. The roofs of Incan dwellings were made of thatch tied to projecting stone knobs at the gable ends (below). Following page, a view from Huayna Picchu.

Machu Picchu Peru

On the evening of November 16, 1532, the Inca Atahualpa was borne into the town square of Cajamarca in the Peruvian Andes near the northern end of his domain. Eighty lords wearing gold and silver headdresses carried his gold-encrusted litter, while lesser nobles, chanting in unison, cleared the paved road before him. The Inca, considered to be a descendant of the Sun, had no apprehensions about the strangers he was going to receive. Thousands of warriors accompanied him; some seventy thousand of his most highly trained soldiers, armed with lances, clubs, slings, and battle-axes, were camped just outside the town. It was a confident, victorious army, as Atahualpa had just won a civil war against his brother's forces, which made him the undisputed master of an empire that stretched for more than three thousand miles north and south along the Andes Mountains.

Undisputed, that is, except by the 150 alien, bearded invaders who, on his invitation, awaited him in Cajamarca. Atahualpa knew that Francisco Pizarro and his band of treasure-seeking conquistadors had looted and devastated the countryside on their march south. He was impressed by the unfamiliar animals they sat upon and their mysterious, loud weapons. But the foreigners professed friendship, and they were too few to represent any true threat. After all, Atahualpa had only to utter a single word to annihilate the whole company.

But Pizarro acted first. Awed by the sophistication of the empire they had stumbled upon and terrified by the size of the army that they had been lured to approach, Pizarro and his captains prepared a desperate ambush. When the Inca threw down a prayer book offered to him by a Dominican friar, Pizarro gave the signal.

Spaniards on horseback charged the native troops, and Spaniards on foot fired their harquebuses. Pizarro himself helped to drag Atahualpa from his litter and hustle him away while the panic-stricken Indians in the square were being slaughtered around them.

At that moment the mighty Incan empire fell, intact, into Spanish hands. Ironically, Atahualpa was destroyed by his own divinity and omnipotence. His rule had become so bureaucratic that not one of his subjects dared give the obvious command to kill the attackers and rescue the king. Pizarro ordered the Inca to disperse his army, and the soldiers dutifully obeyed.

Atahualpa tried to ransom his life by ordering his subjects to bring the Spaniards a roomful of gold. The conquistadors accepted the gold but killed Atahualpa anyway, after a farcical trial which found the Inca guilty of polygamy, idolatry, and his brother's murder. A puppet Inca was installed on the throne, so that the empire continued to function while the Spaniards pillaged its cities and temples. The puppet Inca eventually rebelled and fled to a remote mountain stronghold, where for forty years he and his heirs maintained the fiction of their former power, which they periodically tried to regain. The Spaniards ultimately penetrated even this final retreat and killed the last Inca.

But there was one Incan city the Spaniards never found. It was built just before the conquest, at the height of Incan power, apparently as a refuge or a resort for the Inca himself. Since the Incas had no written records, the name of the city is unknown, as are its builders and their reasons for creating such an inaccessible city on the granite ridge high above the rapids of the Urubamba River. Nor is it known when the city was abandoned. Thousands of Andean workers must have labored for years to haul the huge granite blocks across the steep slopes, just as thousands more must have been employed growing

The Incan highways were carried over the great ravines of the Andes by swaying suspension bridges of vines and fiber ropes (left). The Incas failed to cut all these bridges when the Spaniards arrived, and Pizarro and his cavalry managed to cross several of them. Above, a ritual costume depicted in an Incan embroidery.

Right, Bingham's map of Machu Picchu. Below, a royal messenger alerting the next runner to accept the quipu, *a knotted string (below right) used for accounting.*

corn and potatoes on the narrow terraces cut into the mountain side. Yet, no testimony to its splendor survived, nor was any mention made of it in the many annals of the Spanish conquest. For nearly four hundred years, the empty city slumbered, forgotten.

Hundreds of years after the city was founded, a young American explorer (and, later, a U.S. senator from Connecticut) named Hiram Bingham set out to find the capital of the last Inca. On July 24, 1911, Bingham followed an Indian boy up the steep sides of Machu Picchu mountain. Nine thousand feet above sea level, they crossed a great flight of stone-faced agricultural terraces and entered a dark forest. Bingham wrote later in his book, *Lost City of the Incas*:

Suddenly, I found myself confronted with the walls of ruined houses built of the finest quality of Incan stonework. . . . On top of a ledge was a semicircular building whose outer wall, gently sloping and slightly curved, bore a striking resemblance to the famous Temple of the Sun in Cuzco. This might also be a Temple of the Sun. It followed the natural curvature of the rock and was . . . tied into another beautiful wall, made of very carefully matched ashlars of pure white granite, especially selected

Left, a Spanish print of Pizarro's arrival in South America in 1530. In this depiction, the natives are both fleeing from the Spaniards in terror and offering them gifts of gold and silver.

for its fine grain. . . .

After climbing a stairway of massive granite blocks, Bingham came upon "the most interesting structures in ancient America. Made of beautiful white granite, the walls contained blocks of cyclopean size, higher than a man." These were three-sided temples, facing what Bingham called the Sacred Plaza. One of the temples contained "three great windows looking out over the canyon to the rising sun. Like its neighbor, it is unique among Incan ruins. . . ."

To Bingham, a student of Andean history and lore, the Temple of the Three Windows was particularly fascinating. According to Incan legend set down by the early Spanish chroniclers, the line of Incan rulers was founded by one Manco Capac,

Below, two Incan drawings dating from after the Spanish conquest, depicting the seasons of planting and harvesting.

who came out of the mountains around A.D. 1200 and captured the plateau of Cuzco, thus initiating the long series of Incan conquests. The chronicle states that Manco Capac later returned to his birthplace where he constructed "a masonry wall with three windows," the symbol of the house of his fathers.

Bingham eventually came to believe that the city on Machu Picchu was the original home of the Incan dynasty. Today, it is known, however, that the city was built centuries after Manco Capac's reign. Bingham also believed that in Machu Picchu he had found Vilcabamba, the refuge to which the last Incas fled some years after Pizarro's conquest, bringing with them the Virgins of the Sun. These Incan "nuns" were considered the sun god's earthly brides and, as such, were second in importance only to the Inca. In the 1960s, some long-lost Spanish documents were discovered, proving that some of the conquistadors did, in fact, enter

Vilcabamba and identifying it as another ruin that had already been discovered.

In any case, Machu Picchu was clearly a royal city, a sanctuary where priests "tied" the sun to a special carved rock, the Intihuatána. Here, the Inca himself could have worshiped his solar ancestor.

The city appears to have been built as a refuge. It lies well away from the main Incan highways that crisscrossed the Andes. No spot in the Peruvian highlands is better protected by natural bulwarks. The city straddles a ridge between two peaks, both topped with watchtowers. The steep-sided Urubamba gorge, which was impassable until recently when a road was blasted along the river, curves around the northern peak—the sugarloaf of Huayna Picchu—in a 180-degree turn, effectively guarding the city on three sides. Access was from the south, on two paved Incan roads that clung to the sides of the higher peak—Machu Picchu itself. Where the roads converged, a fort commanded the

Believing that the Spaniards would free him, the captured Inca Atahualpa ordered the wealth of many temples and palaces brought to Pizarro (left). Eleven tons of gold, jewelry, and ornaments were melted down—but the treasure did not save the Inca. Below, a native woman, supervised by a Spanish monk.

razor-backed ridge that led to the city's inner wall. A single, narrow gateway led through the wall to the inner city. This gate could be closed and locked by a massive log door lashed to stone cylinders set deep in the wall.

Not only did the walls and gate keep out enemies, but they also served to bar from the inner precincts both the peasants who farmed the terraces and the common soldiers who guarded the approaches to the city. The central part of the city was segmented into wards or compounds, each containing the dwellings of a particular class or clan. The doors of individual houses had no locks, but the compound of each clan was surrounded by a wall and had only one entrance, which could be bolted shut like the main gate of the city. The stonework and particularly the gate fasteners differ slightly from one compound to another. This diversity could reflect in part the fact that the Incas did not create an indigenous civilization but amalgamated and organized a number of well-developed ancient cultures.

There is one architectural pattern, however, that is common to everything the Incas built. From the main gate to the modest niches in the smallest Machu Pic-

chu house, nearly every aperture is a trapezoid, narrower at the top than at the bottom. This gently tapering form is marvelously suited to Incan design, both aesthetically and practically. The Incas had not discovered the arch, so the tapering doorways and windows shortened the distance that had to be bridged by heavy granite lintels. At the same time, the form harmonizes well with the pyramidal shape of the city itself and of the mountains around it.

The design also finds an echo—or perhaps its origin—in the construction of the walls themselves, which were formed by mounting even rows of rectangular ashlars (hewed blocks), each layer consisting of slightly smaller stones than those of the row beneath. This both eased the problem of lifting the topmost stones into place and assured a wall more likely to resist the earthquakes common in that part of the world. The diminishing height of the upper rows imparts a feeling of gracefulness to Incan walls and makes them appear taller than they actually are.

For the retaining walls of the terraces and the outer compound walls—where strength was crucial—the Incas employed a different style of masonry. Instead of

rectangular ashlars laid in even rows, irregularly shaped boulders were fitted together like a gigantic jigsaw puzzle. Although the surface of these walls is smooth, the haphazard mosaic pattern at first suggests a rougher, less sophisticated level of artistry. But close examination reveals that every irregularity of every stone fits precisely into a corresponding irregularity of an adjacent stone. Such perfect joining required the constant supervision of master craftsmen and engineers as well as a large team of laborers who hewed and meticulously fit boulders that weighed several tons.

Those who fit these stones together, and the Inca they obeyed, could not have known that they were building not just a city but a monument to their civilization. Later, their gold and silver would be stolen, and their people virtually enslaved. Timber and thatched roofs and richly woven wools would rot away. But despite the wind and rain and earthquakes, despite the hardwood trees and jungle undergrowth that occupied the city when Hiram Bingham arrived, the magnificently crafted stonework at Machu Picchu did survive to tell us of Incan glory.

Salamanca

Spain

Preceding page, late afternoon view of the Plaza Mayor, the heart of the city of Salamanca. To the left, on the north side of the square is the town hall (ayuntamiento). The building in the middle is the Royal Pavilion (Pabellón Real).

Facing page, the town hall, completed in 1755. Its façade rests on five sturdy arches, which are noticeably loftier than the arcade that surrounds the square, and is divided into sections by a series of pilasters. Note the polychromatic effect of the two tones of rose and blue-gray stone.

Above and right, the arcades that surround the square.

The center of the east side of the Plaza Mayor is occupied by the Royal Pavilion. The plaque on its façade (left) bears a large medallion with the sculptured likeness of King Philip V, under whose patronage the work was executed. The plaque surmounts the head of a lion.

The coat of arms of Salamanca consists of a bull and a bridge and is found in several versions on many buildings throughout the town (below).

The buildings around the four sides of the plaza have, for the most part, the same structure. They are borne on generous arcades which support three additional stories, rhythmically divided from each other by an unbroken series of balconies (below left and facing page, far right). Only the Royal Pavilion and the town hall (facing page, below right) break the continuity of the balconies.

Facing page, right, the upper part of the façade of the Royal Pavilion, which culminates in the royal coat of arms—a design typical of eighteenth-century Spanish architecture.

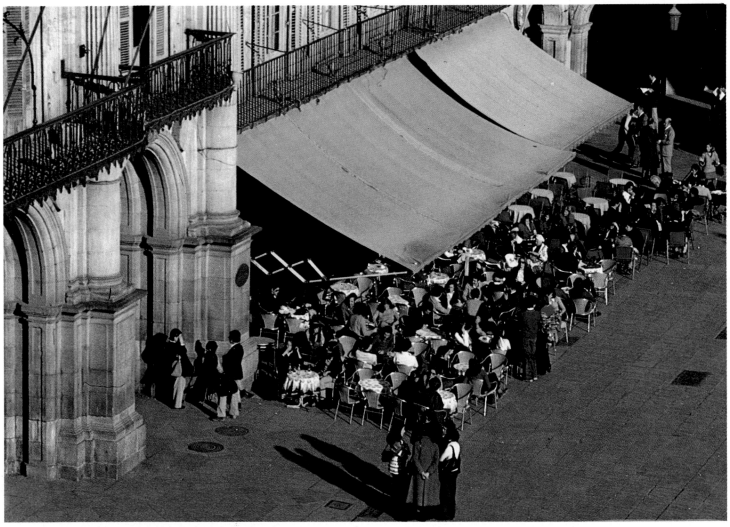

From the colonnade (left) on the south side of the Plaza Mayor, you can cross directly into an adjacent plaza in front of the Church of St. Martin.

Above, a For Rent sign. Most apartments around the square are let to students attending the famous university in the city.

The Plaza Mayor is the center of social life in Salamanca. Here, people bargain for goods (facing page, right) or buy tickets for the National Lottery (far right). Below, students crowd the plaza in front of the town hall, and (below right) townspeople converse at café tables.

The large, sculptured medallions that fill the spaces between the arches surrounding the plaza glorify many of Spain's famous historical figures (facing page, left to right, from top to bottom): Alfonso XI of Castile (1312–1350); Ferdinand of Aragon and Isabella of Castile; Charles II (1661–1700); Philip V (1683–1746); Charles III (1716–1788); Francisco Pizarro; Sancho Davila; Rodrigo Díaz de Bivar (the Cid Campeador); Hernando Cortes; Pérez Correia; Philip II (1527–1598); and Christopher Columbus.

Above, a shield bearing the city's coat of arms. Above right, the bell tower of the town hall, which surmounts the mayor's balcony (right). Below, the bull's head over the central span of the Royal Pavilion.

Following page, the town hall seen from the south end of the plaza.

Salamanca Spain

The Plaza Mayor, or great square, of Salamanca may be the most beautiful in all of Spain. A perfect spot to linger in the cool of the evening, a backdrop for traditional festivities and religious celebrations, it is the true heart of the city. Designed in 1728 by Alberto de Churriguera, the Plaza Mayor combines a French sense of architectural "correctness" and an Italian inventiveness in a characteristically theatrical Spanish setting.

The square is a fitting centerpiece for a city that owes so much of its character to a compatible mixture of European cultures and political influences, which date from the end of the seventeenth century—the time of the Counter Reformation, of interminable wars that lacerated Europe,

and of the founding of colonies by the great powers. The Sun King, Louis XIV, reigned in France, while the Hapsburg monarchs were consolidating their power in Austria.

Those years were difficult ones at the Spanish court. While the other European powers were gathering strength, Spain was still struggling to repay the loans that Charles V and Philip II had borrowed to finance their victorious wars. In addition, the gold coming in from America had unexpectedly upset the economic system instead of putting it to rights. At this time, too, the Spanish branch of the Hapsburg family had become degenerate and sterile. The last Spanish Hapsburg, Charles II, was physically and mentally crippled. Married first to Marie-Louise of Orléans and then to an Austrian princess, Maria Anna of Neuberg, he proved incapable of producing an heir. The powers of Europe were divided over the rival claims to succession of three principal pretenders—France, Austria, and Bavaria.

Eventually, Louis XIV of France succeeded in placing a Bourbon on the Spanish throne—Louis' grandson Philip of Anjou, crowned Philip V of Spain. Nevertheless, Philip was only finally assured the

throne after fourteen years of war, which ended in 1714. Philip was forced to relinquish a sizable portion of his Spanish possessions to guarantee his kingdom. Milan passed to Austria, Minorca to England, and Sicily to the Italian House of Savoy.

Philip did everything in his power to replenish the country's exhausted finances, to reorganize the administration, and to unite the many separate and rebellious provinces that made up Spain at the time. Although he was dedicated to uniting Spain politically, Philip was steadfastly French in taste and education and did much to introduce into Spain the artistic styles then fashionable in his own country.

Though declining politically, Spain was still rich enough to build and ornament splendid cathedrals, and there was great demand for artists to decorate Spain's Baroque churches. Particularly popular forms of ornamentation were the gorgeous retables, enormous structures of carved wood, gilded and painted with flowers, fruits, and figures that formed a backdrop to important altars.

José Simon de Churriguera was an artist from Barcelona who specialized in re-

Left, a nineteenth-century engraving of the Plaza Mayor, the masterpiece of Alberto de Churriguera. He designed the square, considered to be the most beautiful in Spain, in 1728, but it was actually completed in 1755 under the direction of Alberto's student, Andrés García de Quiñones.

Salamanca's skyline is dominated by the majestic church of La Clerecia (left) whose cloisters (below left) are fine examples of the Spanish Renaissance style. Below, one of many drawings by Joachín de Churriguera for the dome of the new cathedral of Salamanca.

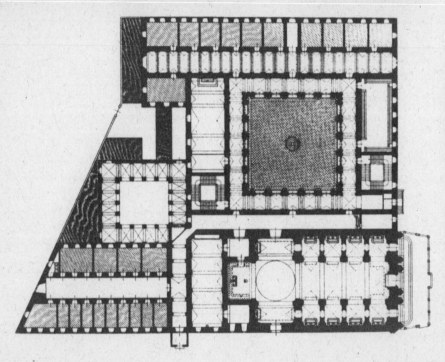

tables. When he fell ill in 1679, he arranged to have his five young sons trained as artists. He died without knowing that he had laid the foundations of a style and a school, known as Churrigueresque, that would last for generations and spread as far as the New World.

All the sons of José Simon de Churriguera were apprenticed to the architect-painters of the court. José Benito, the eldest, was only twenty-four when, in 1689, he won the competition to design the tomb of Queen Marie-Louise. He became assistant designer at the court and quickly established a reputation as an expert at retables.

José Benito soon left Madrid and accepted an official post at Salamanca, where the chapter of the cathedral was seeking an architect to direct the design and construction of the new cathedral. At one time the seat of kings, Salamanca was still a rich and famous city, home of the oldest university in Spain.

José Benito's brothers eventually followed him to Salamanca. In Madrid, where the Churrigueras were close to the court, they had adopted a more Classical architectural style than was current in provincial Salamanca. They had abandoned the exaggerations of the seventeenth century in favor of the international modes, particularly the Classical and linear Roman Baroque, which had been introduced into Spain from France by the Bourbons.

Alberto de Churriguera, who first arrived from Madrid at the age of fourteen and later studied at the university, fell in love with Salamanca. This was the Spain of peaceful provincial towns, far from the political activity at the capital and the luxury of the court. It was, at the same time, a deeply religious Spain that made Holy Week the most important event of the year and put up new domes, new altars, and new churches in honor of the King of Kings.

Every August, the great traditional religious festival, the Feast of the Assumption, was celebrated in and around Salamanca. The festivities that animate and transform the streets today are mere shadows of the celebrations that took place in the seventeenth and eighteenth centuries. In the hot summer months, Alberto and his brothers would start work at dawn, designing and making processional carts, triumphal arches, and backgrounds for the tableaux that were to line the route of the procession. Finally, on the starlit festival night, the townspeople would gather to witness the performance of the *autos sacramentales*—allegorical religious plays—and to listen to Gregorian chants in the wavering light of a thousand candles. After the last notes of the Te Deum died away and the candles had guttered out, the people would emerge from the cathedral in silence. Then, to the sound of one guitar, then another and another, the dancing would begin, and the crowd would be swept up in the music.

Joachín de Churriguera succeeded his brother José Benito as architect of the cathedral, and when Joachín died, Alberto succeeded him in turn. The magnificent stalls of the choir, the sacristy, and the tabernacle of the main altar were all designed by Alberto.

In 1728, as summer approached, Alberto was once again thinking of the preparations for the August celebrations. But he was no longer young, and he was tired of devoting himself to interior decorations and temporary displays. He wanted to leave Salamanca something that would be recognized as his alone, something impressive that would neither be lost in the darkness of the church nor confused with the work of his brothers.

It was not long before he was given his chance. On the evening of July 8, Alberto received a short letter from the governor of Salamanca, Don Rodrigo Caballero, asking if he would be so kind as to call on him briefly the following day. Alberto could not imagine why the civilian governor would want to see the cathedral architect, builder of churches and altars. He supposed the governor might have a request from Madrid for a design for a tomb.

He was offered, however, a surprising commission. He was asked to design a main square for Salamanca—a place for official ceremonies and parades, a place to

The University of Salamanca, founded in the thirteenth century, was for a long time the cultural center of Spain. Tradition has it that Christopher Columbus had to convince the elders of the university that he deserved their support (above).

Left, the late-Gothic façade of the university and the monument to Luis de León, a sixteenth-century poet and religious writer who lived in the city of Salamanca.

receive royalty. At last, Salamanca was to have its Plaza Mayor, and Alberto was able to contribute a masterwork of his own to the city.

Salamanca was already rich in late-Gothic buildings of golden sandstone, in the whorls and flourishes of Baroque architecture, and in the sober lines and delicate ornamentation of the Spanish Renaissance style called Plateresque.

Bounded by the town hall (*ayuntamiento*) on the north and the archway of the Royal Pavilion *(Pabellón Real)* on the east, the Plaza Mayor is approximately square, measuring about 260 feet on each side. At the base of the colonnaded

façades, generous arches span from pier to pier. These have no true capitals; instead, fine medallions between the piers create a delicate and sober accent. Balconies surround the plaza; windows are low and wide, almost square. Above, the façade is crowned by a balustrade as fragile as a Spanish comb, broken by small, carved uprights that form a lacelike pattern of golden sandstone.

The plaza reflects what were, at the time, modern attitudes about architecture. Alberto de Churriguera had rejected the excesses of the Baroque. He preferred to achieve his effects through rhythmic architectural masses rather than decoration. He considered that sculpture should complement—not conceal—architecture.

The native Spanish Baroque style triumphs only in the façade of the Royal Pavilion, where the stone is modeled with some of the fluency and decorative exuberance that was imitated—often to excess—in the style that was later to be called Churrigueresque.

On the medallions between the arches surrounding the plaza, Alberto de Churriguera represented Spain's heritage in his depictions of Ferdinand and Isabella;

Charles V, who claimed that the sun never set upon his dominions; and heroes such as Rodrigo Díaz de Bivar, known in song and story as the Cid Campeador; Hernando Cortes, the conquistador; and Miguel de Cervantes, the author of *Don Quixote de la Mancha*.

In 1738, after disagreements with the conservative cathedral chapter, Churriguera withdrew from his post as architect for Salamanca's new cathedral. He left the

work he had begun on the bell tower for the already consecrated church and devoted himself to directing work on the plaza and building the chapel of the cathedral in Burgos and the Church of St. Anthony in Madrid. He died at Orgaz in the province of Toledo many years before the Plaza Mayor was finished. Adhering faithfully to his master's drawings, Alberto's favorite pupil, Andrés García de Quiñones, completed the work, and the plaza was solemnly inaugurated in 1755.

Since that time, the Plaza Mayor has remained at the core of social life in Salamanca. Until the mid-nineteenth century, it was the site of bullfights. And every evening there was the traditional promenade that is still common in Latin countries, with the men walking in one direction around the square and the women in the other, a practice that made certain everyone could see and be seen.

More than two hundred years later, townspeople, students, and visitors still find the square an agreeable place in which to celebrate, relax, stroll, and converse. A setting of singular charm and beauty, the Plaza Mayor clearly reflects the love of one architect for his adopted city.

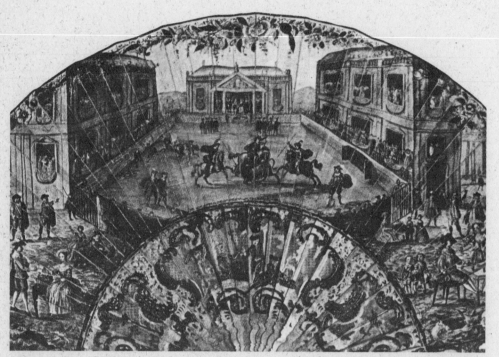

Above left, an antique, painted Spanish fan depicting a bullfight in a plaza. Up until the mid-nineteenth century, such bullfights were held in the Plaza Mayor.

Left, the Plaza Mayor crowded with spectators for a game of chess, played with living pieces in old Spanish costumes.

The Vieux Carré of
New Orleans

U.S.A.

Preceding page, view of the Vieux Carré, showing the symmetric design of the original city as planned by Adrien de Pauger in 1718. In the center is Jackson Square, formerly the Place d'Armes, a parade ground and meeting place. It is flanked by the Pontalba Buildings, constructed in 1850. Facing the river is the St. Louis Cathedral, rebuilt following the fire of 1794 and remodeled in 1851 and, on its right, is the Cabildo, once the seat of the Spanish colonial government.

The sunny streets of the Vieux Carré are celebrated for their weblike ironwork (left) and European flavor. Most buildings are a blend of French, Spanish, and Colonial styles, as are the Pontalba Buildings (far right) and the La Branche Building (below right) at the corner of Royal and St. Peter streets. Right, Pirates Alley, which runs between the cathedral and the Cabildo—a traditional location for sidewalk artists.

The lacy balconies, doors, and gateways of the Vieux Carré are among the loveliest iron architecture in the world. Some date from the years following the great fires of 1788 and 1794, when the Creole, or New Orleans, style of building was developed. Others are modern examples. Early works, such as the detail from a railing at the Bosque House (1795) (near right), in which the owner had his initials entwined in the pattern, are of finely worked wrought iron. Later buildings (right, center row) used a more ornate cast iron, which was usually painted black or white to prevent rust. Motifs such as the morning glory, the live oak, and the rose vine were introduced by local artisans.

One of the most attractive aspects of Creole architecture is its courtyards, hidden away behind high brick walls (left) and dim carriage ways. Buildings, constructed of cypress timber and brick, were usually L-shaped, creating a natural courtyard. Brick or flagstone paving and borders of bougainvillea and hibiscus, which create a cool, airy retreat from the semitropical climate, reflect a Spanish influence.

Fountains such as the ones in the courtyards of Seignouret House and Beauregard House (below left and below) contribute to a lush, tranquil environment.

Facing page, an arched entrance way and ironwork gate typical of early nineteenth-century homes in New Orleans. The shuttered windows keep the rooms cool.

The Beauregard House, built in 1826, exempli-
fies the "raised cottage," in which the living
quarters appear above a basement built at
ground level to avoid flooding. Originally owned
by the LeCarpentier family, the house was the
birthplace of Paul Morphy, a world champion
chess player in the mid-nineteenth century, and
was briefly occupied by the Confederate Civil
War general, P. G. T. Beauregard. Above left,
the austere desk of Louisiana supreme court
justice Alonzo Morphy, a native of Spanish and
British stock, who married Mademoiselle Le-
Carpentier, owner of the house. In the bedroom
(above) tall windows opposite the canopied bed
provide maximum air circulation as well as a
frame for the oval portrait of the owner. Wide
fanlight windows and French doors in the dining
room (left) open out onto the gallery of the
courtyard.

Facing page, interior views of the Beauregard
House. The plaster ceiling rosette and carved
marble mantel of the formal room (right) are
typical of the Greek Revival architecture of the
period, as are the plaster moldings. The style of
the fireplace is classically simple (above, far
right). The music on the piano (above right) recalls the memory of Madame Beauregard.

Following page, a picturesque view of the Vieux
Carré, renowned for its wrought ironwork.

The Vieux Carré of New Orleans U.S.A.

For most of us, the name New Orleans evokes romantic images of an exotic city unlike any other in the United States. We picture the exuberant celebration of the Mardi Gras, when the streets are filled with fantastic floats and bizarrely clad dancers revel far into the night. Or we imagine scenes from the past: languid, black-haired beauties slowly fanning themselves on lacy balconies while Mississippi steamboats drift past, bearing their cargoes of cardsharps and brass bands.

For jazz enthusiasts, New Orleans means Buddy Bolden, King Oliver, Jelly Roll Morton, Louis Armstrong, and hundreds of other musicians who played in smoky barrooms or made their names while "tailgating" trombone on the bandwagons that rolled through the city streets. And for gourmets, New Orleans means gumbo, creole rice, pompano en papillote, and jambalaya—recipes created from a pleasing mixture of French, Spanish, African, and Caribbean cuisines. It also brings to mind the Cajuns and the bayous of southern Louisiana, and the once-common native Afro-French dialect, sometimes called "gumbo ya-ya."

The romantic character of New Orleans's past—a rich potpourri of races and cultures—lingers on today despite the city's busy port and thriving chemical industry. It is only necessary to cross Canal Street, which divides the old city from the new, to discover the heart of New Orleans: the Vieux Carré, also called the French Quarter. Here, time seems to have slowed. The narrow streets, flanked by brick and plaster houses often dating from the eighteenth and early nineteenth centuries, are reminiscent of the colonial past, and the active life of the area has a distinctly cosmopolitan atmosphere.

The Vieux Carré, which constituted the original city of New Orleans, was founded in 1718 by Jean-Baptiste le Moyne, sieur de Bienville, as part of an attempt to establish and consolidate France's holdings in this part of North America. In 1682, the French explorer La Salle had claimed for his country all the land drained by the Mississippi and its tributaries, naming it Louisiana after Louis XIV. Bienville astutely recognized the potential for a port in this area, and in 1699, he insured a French future for the city. He tricked the captain of an English expeditionary fleet into believing that a large French naval force lay beyond a bend in the river, with the consequence that the English abandoned their attempt to seize the area. Bienville then christened the city Nouvelle Orléans in honor of Philippe II, the Duke of Orléans, who was regent of France during the minority of Louis XV.

The plan for the new town was drawn up by assistant royal engineer Adrien de Pauger. De Pauger planned a rectangular city, fronting on the river and surrounded by walls, with a central square—the Place d'Armes, now Jackson Square. A uniform

Left, a nineteenth-century engraving of New Orleans, depicting the busy traffic on the Mississippi.

Below, river boats being unloaded at port. Such boats linked the producers of the Midwest and West with Eastern and European markets.

however, the land was reclaimed for Spain by General Alexander O'Reilly, a soldier in the Spanish army, and New Orleans settled down to enjoy thirty years of peaceful Spanish rule. The city prospered and grew in sophistication. Trade with Europe was greatly expanded, agriculture was encouraged, and new waves of immigrants arrived—among them the Acadians, or Cajuns, who were French settlers ex-

checkerboard of streets divided the area into sixty-six, 300-foot-square blocks. The surrounding walls were destroyed in the early nineteenth century, but de Pauger's grid of perfectly square city blocks remains intact.

Although New Orleans became the capital of Louisiana in 1722, its earliest inhabitants were largely criminals and social misfits who were sent from France in response to Bienville's request for settlers. Gradually, however, more responsible members of society made their way to the new colony. Immigrants arrived from the Caribbean and from France, slaves were brought from Africa, and John Law, owner of the powerful Company of the West, imported hard-working German

peasants to populate his land. Language difficulties often led to permanent misunderstandings, as in the case of one Johann Zweig, who grew so frustrated at a French clerk's inability to understand his name that he tore a twig from a tree and brandished it, shouting, "Zweig! Zweig!" The Frenchman beamed. "Ah! La Branche!" he replied, and promptly entered Zweig's name on the record as La Branche.

In 1763, the area west of the Mississippi and the "Isle of Orleans" were secretly ceded to Spain under the Treaty of Paris at the end of the Seven Years' War. When the city's French inhabitants learned of this betrayal four years later, they were understandably indignant and deposed the first governor sent from Spain. In 1769,

pelled from Nova Scotia by the British in 1755.

French culture remained dominant, although a Spanish influence began to make itself known in cooking, in social life, and especially in architecture. After the great fires of 1788 and 1794, large sections of New Orleans were rebuilt. These houses, constructed of bricks and cypress timbers and stuccoed to meet the new fire regulations, were in a unique, indigenous style. They retained the French custom of closing their buildings around a courtyard for privacy, but Spanish balconies, or galleries, were added to improve air circulation, and the use of the delicate ironwork that has become a symbol of New Orleans was adopted. The style, which today is seen throughout the Vieux Carré, was ideally suited to the hot, damp climate of the city.

New Orleans never really became Spanish, but neither did it remain French. In 1801, another secret agreement returned Louisiana to French rule, but before the colonists could react to this news, they found themselves under the American flag. Less than a month after France took possession, Napoleon sold the troublesome territory to President Thomas Jefferson. English became the official language of the city, and the Creole inhabitants—descendants of the original French and Spanish settlers—greatly resented the imposition of a Protestant, republican, Anglo-Saxon government on their essentially Catholic, monarchist, European community.

Despite the initial hostility of the Creole population, the city experienced its greatest period of growth after it came under the control of the United States. Commerce increased enormously, and Mississippi river boats were kept busy transporting sugar and the new crop, cotton, which would profoundly affect Southern life.

By 1840, the population of New Orleans had doubled. With 100,000 people, it was the fourth largest city in the United States. Many of the new inhabitants were slaves, brought from the West Indies, Senegal, Guinea, and the Congo to work in the cotton industry.

New Orleans had always had a sub-

stantial black population, composed of many "free people of color" as well as slaves. But with the arrival of so many new blacks, the social structure changed. Superstition and voodoo became more prevalent, as did the intricate rhythms of African music. In time, it became customary for blacks to gather on Sundays and holidays in Congo Square (now Beauregard Square) where they listened to the drums or danced the slow, throbbing *bamboula*.

In fact, dancing was a way of life for everyone in New Orleans, black and white. Balls were so popular that, when the American commissioner, William C. C. Claiborne, arrived in 1803, he reported to Secretary of State James Madison that

Rafts were used to transport timber down the Mississippi (above), but the steamboat was the most popular form of transportation. Card players often gathered in the grand salons (below) to play poker during the long voyages.

a major problem in his first six weeks was to reassure leading citizens that the ballrooms would not be closed, since fights were erupting over whether to play French or American dances. These disputes were apparently settled, as balls—particularly the quadroon balls, which were attended only by white men and respectable young women of color, and masked balls, where birth, wealth, and color made no difference—continued to be popular.

By 1838, dancing had begun to spill out onto the streets, and New Orleans became a city of parades. Almost any excuse was enthusiastically approved. Mardi Gras had been celebrated in the town since the day the French arrived in 1699 and became a public event with floats and masks in 1838. Weddings and business openings were celebrated with band music and dancing. Curiously, a festive ritual even developed for funerals. On the way to the cemetery, the mourners would slowly follow a band playing a dirge, but on the way back to town, the band would change its beat. The mourners, now relieved of their burden, danced to accompany the freed soul on its way to Heaven.

Naturally enough, with so many occasions calling for dancing and parades, New Orleans began to attract musicians, and it soon became the music capital of the country. Its opera was renowned, especially during the 1840s and 1850s, and provided many opportunities for all to hear the finest contemporary European compositions. After the Civil War, however, brass bands dominated the musical life of New Orleans. Bandwagons rolled up Bourbon Street, down Basin Street, and across Canal Street, providing free entertainment while advertising local businesses and coming events. "Cutting contests," when one band would try to outplay another, were proving grounds for many young musicians, and early jazz men such as King Oliver and Freddie Keppard made their names in these impromptu competitions. It is said that Keppard was so jealous of his reputation as the top trumpeter in New Orleans that he covered his right hand with a handkerchief when he played so no one could imitate his technique.

By the end of the nineteenth century, New Orleans had a reputation as a good-time town, a name derived not only from its music but also from its prostitutes. In 1897, the town fathers adopted a plan, introduced by Alderman Sidney Story, to restrict the ladies to an area of thirty-eight blocks. Storyville, as the district came to be called, was soon the most celebrated red-light district in America. Each prostitute was listed in the *Blue Book,* an official guide to elegant establishments such as Mahogany Hall, run by the diamond-encrusted Lulu White, and Château Lobrano d'Arlington, managed by the mistress of Storyville's unofficial mayor.

The brothels of Storyville are traditionally credited with being the birthplace of jazz, though, in fact, the musical form had already developed before the district was created. Many musicians—especially pianists such as Jelly Roll Morton—did find work in the lounges and bars of the area, but when Storyville was closed in 1917, they moved to other cities in search of jobs. One white band, the Original Dixieland Jazz Band, made its way to New York, where it recorded the first jazz record and touched off a worldwide craze.

New Orleans was slow to accept the fact that it had created the "only original American art form." The *Times-Picayune* remarked in 1918 that, "As far as jass (sic) and jassism is concerned New Orleans has a particular interest, seeing that it is widely said that this sort of musical vice was born in this city, and that in fact it originated in our streets of shame. We do not accept the honor of this parenthood, but as this story is in circulation we must make sure that we are the last to welcome this atrocity into respectable society." The spirit of Bourbon Street prevailed, however, and today there are many monuments to jazz in the Vieux Carré.

The music, like so much in this unique city, is rooted in traditions from all over the world—the *bamboula* of Congo Square, parade music, French dances, Italian opera, West Indian folk music. But the result is pure New Orleans: a sensuous, felicitous blend of seemingly disparate cultural ingredients.

Although the danger of explosion could lead to scenes like the one at left, steamboat races were a highlight of river life during the mid-nineteenth century. Below, a race between the Natchez *and the* Eclipse, *two large paddle boats which carried passengers and cotton up and down the Mississippi.*

James Joyce's Dublin

Ireland

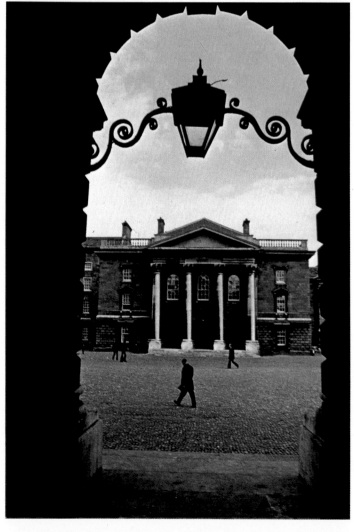

Preceding page, City Quay, near the mouth of the River Liffey. This is a landscape which often recurs in the pages of Joyce. These pages, the chief monuments of "official" Dublin. Left, the Custom House, built in 1781 in the Neoclassical style by the English architect James Gandon. Below left, two views of Trinity College, founded in Elizabeth I's reign in an effort to "civilize" Ireland. Above, seal on the front gate of St. Patrick's Cathedral, founded by the first Norman Archbishop of Dublin. Right, City Hall, originally Dublin's Royal Exchange. Below, Protestant Christ Church Cathedral, built between 1176 and 1230 on the site of an old Norse cathedral.

Today, more than seventy years after Joyce wrote Dubliners, *Dublin remains a city full of contradictions, deeply rooted in its Catholic and Gaelic past and slowly coming to grips with the realities of the modern industrial world. With its ancient quays, elegant brick façades, and dreary slums, contemporary Dublin is recognizably Joyce's Dublin, and the visitor can wander around the same streets that Joyce's Dubliners once haunted.*

Dublin today, as in Joyce's time, is a city of many pubs. Its largest industry is the production of stout, and the generous amount consumed locally is legendary. Dublin's public houses function as neighborhood centers where locals gather to exchange stories and news. There are workers' pubs and bankers' pubs, and rarely does one find a man without a pub to call his own.

With a map and a red pencil, Joyce charted the movements of his characters through the streets of Dublin and beyond them to the sea. At times comforting "like a great sweet mother" and at other moments hostile, the sea provides a setting for many crucial scenes in his works. By the sea, the young Stephen Dedalus has a radiant vision of a bird girl, a vision that inspires him to become an artist. Ulysses opens with Stephen at the Martello Tower (facing page), where Joyce lived for a while. Built as a fortification during the Napoleonic Wars, the tower—now the James Joyce Museum—symbolizes the isolation of the artist. Following page, Joyce's birthplace, 41 Brighton Square, Rathgar.

James Joyce's Dublin Ireland

Of all the Irishmen of letters who have immortalized their love for Ireland in their works, none springs to mind more readily than James Joyce. Although Joyce left Ireland as soon as he could, he never ceased to write about it, and particularly about his native city of Dublin. Indeed, his earliest work was a collection of short stories entitled *Dubliners*. These stories provide revealing insights into the inhabitants of Joyce's Dublin.

Joyce's greatest work, *Ulysses,* is even more factually accurate about the city he knew as a youth. Joyce himself would claim that, should Dublin be destroyed, his *Ulysses* could provide the guide for its reconstruction—just as the nineteenth-century German archaeologist Heinrich Schliemann was able to identify the ruins of Troy by tracking down references to the ancient city in the copy of Homer's *Iliad,* trusting that Homer's epic was based on fact.

Joyce went to great pains to insure the veracity of his work, and he often wrote to Dublin relatives from various places of exile on the Continent to inquire about some place or character from his youth, some name or date. With a red pen and ruler, he actually charted the epic wanderings of his modern-day Ulysses, Leopold Bloom, through the streets, houses, pubs, and monuments of the city.

Joyce's *Ulysses* depicts a Dublin that readers relive when they wander its narrow, picturesque streets. Many visitors cannot explore the parks, the quays, and the pubs without recalling the story of Leopold and Molly Bloom and Stephen Dedalus and recognizing the vitality of the Dubliners Joyce portrayed. Joyce's very tangible descriptions of Dublin—the Georgian houses with their front steps down to the pavement, the red-brown brick façades, the barges on the river, the lingering scent of incense in the churches, the huge pats of butter in the grocers' shops—evoke a particular city at a particular time. But Joyce's intent was not merely journalistic accuracy—his Dublin was literary, a city that had a kinship with Homer. Thus, Joyce's *Ulysses* is a twentieth-century version of Homer's *Odyssey,* full of allusions to the Greek epic.

The Martello Tower, where *Ulysses*

Above, James Joyce with his daughter Lucia.

Right, Magaline Hill, one of the settings in Ulysses.

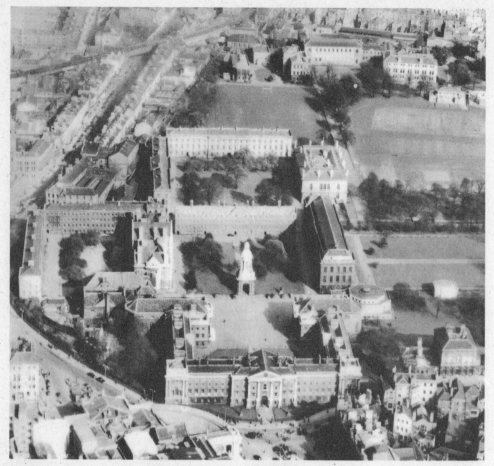

Above, an aerial view of Trinity College.

Two examples of ancient Irish art. Above, a page in the "Book of Kells," an eighth-century illuminated manuscript of the Gospels. Right, the twelfth-century reliquary of St. Patrick's bell.

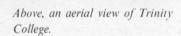

opens, is an actual Dublin landmark, one of a series of towers built as coastal fortifications throughout the British Isles at the time of the Napoleonic Wars. It is also a place where Joyce lived for a while, and in the novel, it is the home of the aesthete Stephen Dedalus—but the connection is more than literal. On one level, the tower corresponds to the lodgings of Ulysses' son, Telemachus, who lived "in the tower" of his father's house. In its resemblance to Elsinore's haunted battlements, it echoes young Stephen's comparison of himself with Shakespeare's Hamlet. And in the larger contexts of modern Irish literature and modern symbolist poetry, the tower is a favorite image of the artist's lonely but privileged viewpoint.

By using symbolism in this way, Joyce imbues his private view of Dublin with a universal meaning and import. He combines a timeless Classical sense with the distinctive detail of the modern city, at once sordid and sublime.

It has often been said that Joyce had to leave Dublin to describe it better, to depict narratives and characters there with a more exact, dispassionate eye. Joyce spent his adult life away from Ireland, returning only once for a brief visit. He lived for many years in Trieste, Italy, where his children were born. He was married in London, finally legalizing his twenty-seven-year relationship with his common-law wife Nora Barnacle. During World War I, he lived in Zurich, where he died in 1941.

Joyce's feelings toward Dublin were paradoxical and complex. For him it was "dear dirty Dublin," an alliteration that exposes his ambivalence about the city. He loved it, but the naturalistic writer in him could not ignore its squalor. "It isn't my fault," he said once, "if the smell of ashes, rotten weeds, and rubbish hovers around my stories." And yet the moralist—or perhaps more correctly the aesthete—in him also condemned Dubliners and the Irish as a race of "clodhoppers."

In much the same way that Dante—one of Joyce's inspirations and fellow exiles—judged the Florentines, casting them in

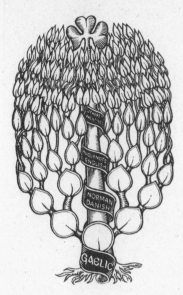

Above, a reconstruction of the genealogical tree of the Gaelic people.

Above, the Heraldic Museum and the Bedford Tower, both part of Dublin Castle. The castle, sections of which date from the thirteenth century, served as the seat of the English Lord Lieutenant until 1922. Below, the Martello Tower.

the latitude and longitude of Stephen Dedalus and Mr. Bloom as they stand outside the house at 7 Eccles Street. He vividly recounts the details of student life at Trinity College, a Protestant institution dating back to 1592, and observes the singular position of priests and Jesuits in a city split by religion.

Joyce's works describe the Ancient Concert Room, where he had once sung in his fine tenor; the O'Connell Bridge; the small islands at the estuary of the River Liffey; Belvedere College, stronghold of the Jesuits with whom Joyce studied; Kildare Street, with its National Library; and Leinster House and the Royal College of Physicians.

In his most formidable work, *Finnegans Wake,* Joyce transforms a few episodes in such familiar Dublin locales as Finns Hotel and Phoenix Park into an epic written in a new Joycean language. In this novel, the River Liffey is central to the theme, just as it is the pulse of Dublin itself. Dublin is named after its river. The word comes from the Gaelic *dubh linn,* meaning "black pool." Joyce's use of "riverrun" as a metaphor for history is, therefore, particularly appropriate.

Indeed, *Finnegans Wake,* like the Liffey, enters the heart of Dublin, touching landmarks as it flows along its way. The river, also called Anna Liffey, suggests the heroine of the book, Anna Livia Plura-

hell or elevating them to heaven, Joyce judges Dublin. Referring to it as "the paralysis that many call a city," he both rewards and punishes its inhabitants. But while on the surface he remains cool, detached, and ironic, his passion is revealed by his frequent and exacting descriptions of people, places, and customs he remembered from his early years in Dublin.

These details range from curious town characters like Hoppy Holohan, with his game leg, to Charles Stewart Parnell, the political figure, and include 7 Eccles Street, the address of a friend, which Joyce made Leopold Bloom's address in *Ulysses.* Joyce preserves them for all time, while endowing them with broader meaning. Even the smallest things can be crucial. Ironically, Joyce liked nothing better than to imagine future scholars pursuing the meaning of some offhand mention of Dublin's bookies or local beers.

In a section of *Ulysses* entitled "In the Heart of the Hibernian Metropolis," Joyce lists the names and destinations of trams leaving the center of Dublin. (One such destination is the suburb of Rathgar, Joyce's birthplace.) Humorously, he gives

belle. At the same time, it personifies the streams of thought and language that flow through Joyce's consciousness. "Riverrun" is the first word in the book, and also the last, since the structure of the book was meant to define a circle, with the last word harking back to the beginning—a cycle that recalls the continuous flow of the river.

The city's history, as well as its landmarks, provides a wealth of references in Joyce's work. Converted to Christianity by Saint Patrick in the fifth century, the city was taken by the Vikings and used as a stronghold and base for raiding missions. It was reconquered by the Irish under Brian Boru and then taken by the Normans in the early twelfth century. It was a long-time seat of conflict between Catholics and Protestants, both of whom maintained a bishop there.

If at times Joyce eagerly satirized the

Leopold Bloom's "voyage" in Ulysses *takes him to Sackville Street in central Dublin, shown here as it looked in 1885. In the background is the tall Nelson's Column, recently destroyed by Irish nationalists.*

city of his birth, his positive feelings toward it emerge occasionally in the form of exaggeration. He once bragged that Dublin had been "a capital for thousands of years, the second city of the British Empire, three times as big as Venice." The first claim had lost whatever truth it had once possessed by 1800 when the Act of Union carried Irish government to London, the second would provoke snickers all over England, and the third is undermined when it is considered that size was hardly Venice's claim to fame. But the statement does show the affection that existed alongside Joyce's ridicule of the Sinn Feiners (members of the Irish national movement) and the conservative middle classes, whom he called respectively "Their Intensities" and "Their Calfships."

The years have in some ways borne out the truth of Joyce's criticism. The city he grew up in has allowed many of its splendid Georgian buildings to fall into disrepair. Political and religious strife has scarred the face of the city. In 1916, insurgent nationalists burned out the inside of the General Post Office, "a symbol of foreign dominance," and fifty years later

extremists bombed the nearby Nelson's Column for the same reason.

The city's reaction to Joyce himself, Dublin's famous literary offspring, has only slowly and grudgingly changed from resentment to pride. For many years, Joyce was considered a deserter and ungrateful son of Ireland. The Bloomsday celebration held every June 16 is a custom of recent origin. Irish pride is not the most forgiving, even though the memory of Joyce is a potentially lucrative lure for tourists. Like prophets of all sorts—including Homer himself, who went hungry in the famous seven cities that later competed to claim him as a native son—Joyce may have to wait until the time he predicted, when a Dublin in ruins will have to turn to his books for clues to its own reconstruction. That could be history's justice.

But by that time, the real Dublin, like Troy before it, will long since have become myth. We will no longer be able to see the city except through Joyce's eyes, as we can no longer view Troy except through Homer's. Joyce tried to contain the entire world in microcosm within Dublin. His books may well encompass Dublin in the same way.